THE UNOFFICIAL BUSINESS TRAVELER'S POCKET GUIDE

THE UNOFFICIAL BUSINESS TRAVELER'S POCKET GUIDE

165 Tips Even the Best Business Travelers May Not Know

CHRISTOPHER J. McGINNIS

McGraw-Hill

New York • San Francisco • Washington, D.C. • Auckland
Bogotá • Caracas • Lisbon • London • Madrid • Mexico City
Milan • Montreal • New Delhi • San Juan • Singapore
Sydney • Tokyo • Toronto

Library of Congress Cataloging-in-Publication Data

McGinnis, Christopher J.
The unofficial business traveler's pocket guide : 165 tips even the best business travelers may not know / by Christopher McGinnis.
p. cm.
ISBN 0-07-045380-2
1. Business travel—Guidebooks. I. Title.
G168.6.B86M384 1998
91n'2'02—dc21 98–13844
CIP

McGraw-Hill
A Division of The McGraw-Hill Companies

1 2 3 4 5 6 7 8 9 0 FGR/FGR 9 0 3 2 1 0 9 8

ISBN 0-07-045380-2

The sponsoring editor for this book was Jeffrey Krames, the editing supervisor was Donna Namorato, and the production supervisor was Suzanne W. B. Rapcavage. It was set in Melior by Lisa M. King of Editorial and Production Services.

Printed and bound by Quebecor Fairfield.

This book is printed on recycled paper.

To Julia, who gave me two most important gifts: observation and communication

CONTENTS

Introduction ix
Acknowledgments xv

PART ONE

THE TRIP

1 Things to Know Before You Go 3
2 What to Bring and How to Bring It 27
3 Getting to and from the Airport 37
4 Surviving the Airport 53
5 On the Plane 79
6 On the Road 101
7 At the Hotel 117
8 Using the Telephone 139

PART TWO

GENERAL INFORMATION

9 Frequent Traveler Programs 155
10 International Travel 173
11 Eating Well 201
12 Your Heart, Your Mind, and Your Body 217

APPENDIX 233
INDEX 239

INTRODUCTION

While business travelers come from hundreds of different countries, speak many different languages, and work for thousands of different companies, we have a culture and lifestyle as unique as that of the traveling Gypsies.

Think about it. When we are on the road, we all pretty much read the same magazines and newspapers, wear the same clothes, and have the same problems balancing work life and family life. We eat the same food, stay at the same hotels, and endure the same long flights in cramped quarters. We even recognize each other in ways that outsiders are not able to see. And we also hoard and spend the same currency—the frequent flier mile.

In 1984 I took my first business trip, an induction of sorts to this class of "commercial nomad." I had just completed the master's program at the American Graduate School of International Management ("Thunderbird") in Phoenix, Arizona. Sea-Land, the containerized shipping company, invited me to New York for a job interview.

I remember the feeling of importance I had when booking my airline ticket through their company travel agency. The agent reserved a room for me at the Holiday Inn "Jetport" at Newark Airport. The company even thought enough of me to express-mail the tickets to Arizona the following day. Wow! This was the big time! Bright-eyed and eager, I must have read over my itinerary, tickets, and boarding passes at least a dozen times.

When the big day arrived, I packed a suit in my hang-up bag, put my résumé in my briefcase, and headed off to the airport. This time I wasn't flying home for the holidays or away on spring break. This was a business trip! A bit apprehensive about this new role, I watched the briefcase and trench coat crowd for cues: look straight ahead, walk fast, keep a pen in your pocket, feign indifference, don't check your bag, do some work on the plane, and generally, act serious.

I arrived at my hotel in Newark at dusk. In my room overlooking the runways, I watched planes take off into the sunset, ate a room service club sandwich, pondered life, and worried about my interview. Little did I know that this transcontinental trip and Holiday Inn stay would be much more meaningful to my true calling than the impending interview.

Not that I didn't get the job with Sea-Land. I did, and it was with them that I took my first steps as a business traveler. However, the frequent traveling really began when I accepted my second job as a trainer with a management consulting company. That job demanded travel every Sunday night through Friday night.

For the next three years, I lived on airplanes and at airports, stayed at hundreds of hotels, drove thousands of miles in rental cars, made countless long-distance credit card calls, missed my family and friends, and got hooked on the then-nascent frequent traveler programs. I soon found that I was much more enamored of the travel industry than the consulting business. Naturally, I became my company's resident travel guru.

The company had a reputation for inducting young Turks from business schools, chewing them up for a couple of years, and spitting them out. Exit interviews showed that most of those who quit left because of "the travel." Having doled out mountains of advice to the semi-annual class of new recruits, or "green peas," I suggested to management that part of our company's training program be devoted to teaching the art of frequent travel: in other words, a traveler training program.

Business travelers no longer flew from city A to city B, did their job, then flew home. With airline deregulation, the frequent traveler marketplace had exploded and everything had become negotiable. Telephones and long-distance calling were different, airline travel was a maze of new fares, rules, restrictions, hubs, and spokes. Hotels offered unheard-of choices like concierge levels and video check-out. Credit cards changed, and car rental contracts became fine-print gobbledygook.

To me, it was obvious. Business travelers everywhere needed help. For many companies and individuals, learning how to travel on the job was the hard, expensive way. At just about that time, Marriott published the results of a survey which concluded that although companies were spending almost $100 billion a year on travel and entertainment, only 5 percent of business travelers had ever received any formal training on how to make travel better. And almost all of them thought that training would definitely yield benefits.

Reading that survey in *USA Today* on a flight to Bozeman, Montana, pushed me over the edge. I would do it on my own. So I quit the consulting company and launched Travel Skills Group in 1988. Since then we have kept travelers up to date and in the know through traveler training programs, newspaper and magazine columns, and regular TV and radio segments. My first book, *202*

Tips Even the Best Business Travelers May Not Know, published in 1994, has made it into the hands of over 35,000 people. And since that book came out, a lot has changed.

Hotel chains are updating rooms and adding business traveler-friendly amenities. Robust airlines are buying newer planes, installing bigger, more comfortable seats in business class, improving food, and experimenting with technologically advanced in-flight entertainment systems. Airport clubs are getting a makeover; they are now more like high-tech offices compared to the old, smoky-drinky lounges of yesterday. Rental cars are getting technological enhancements like global positioning satellite systems. Even airport restaurants and stores are upgrading their offerings.

This book is an updated version of the last one, and a compendium of much of what we have learned, taught, and advised over the last 10 years. In the coming pages, you will find a one-room-schoolhouse approach, meaning that these tips should be useful to both novice and seasoned travelers.

Everyone will find at least a few aha's and I-never-knew-that's in the coming pages. Anyone who is planning to join or is already in this new world of business travel will benefit from this book's tips and advice. Even business travel industry professionals will find new ideas to pass on to their frequent-traveling customers.

The advice is presented as quickly read, easily grasped and retained tips—useful or interesting nuggets of information to make your life on the road better. Some tips are one-liners. Others cover a number of ideas on a general subject.

Part One, "The Trip," is set up chronologically and covers trip planning, packing, getting to the airport, the flight, the drive, and the hotel stay. Part Two, "General Information," provides tips that you can use at any point in your travels, from foreign currency exchange, to eating alone, to staying fit on the road. Interspersed throughout, you'll find a handful of interesting stories and colorful first-person accounts of business trips to cities around the world. There you'll find out whether or not I follow my own advice and see that I've learned a few things the hard way!

ACKNOWLEDGMENTS

It's surprising how many people helped make this book possible. Here's a stab at giving recognition to a key few.

First, I'd like to thank my readers, those loyal road warriors who since 1988 have followed my work on television or in periodicals like the *Atlanta Journal-Constitution, Fortune, Entrepreneur*, and my homegrown newsletter, *The Ticket*. Readers are some of my top sources; they're like an extra thousand or so eyes and ears. They've helped keep me abreast of an exciting and dynamic market, one that a single travel writer could never cover on his or her own. Thanks for all your calls, letters, e-mails, and across-the-airplane-aisle advice and opinions!

Carving out the time necessary to create this book would never have been possible without the unflagging efforts of my business manager, Catharine Kuchar, and my editorial assistant, Tina Stults. And, thanks to the friendship and advice of business travelers Tony Morris, John Kirtland, and Jeff Dossey, the material that follows is as concise, correct, and useful as possible.

I owe a huge debt to Randy Petersen, whose knowledge of frequent-travel programs is spelled out in Chapter 9. Randy has been a mentor and friend of my newsletter business and opened the door to my participation in periodic *Fortune* magazine special business travel sections. It's good to know I can rely on people like Randy.

I'm equally indebted to my various editors, the ones responsible for making my work accurate and readable. Thanks to Scott Thurston, Jim

Harrison, Joanna Krotz, Karen Axelton, and Chris Smith. And when it comes to TV, it's the producers in CNN's Travel News Unit who have helped keep my comments sharp, my tie straight, and my ego in check. Thanks to Sheila Hula, Chad Kononetz, Kathy Kuczka, Robin McDaniel, Mary Orlin, Stephanie Oswald, Greg Phillips, Kalin Thomas-Samuel, Lori Waffenschmidt and Kim Wiglesworth. And thanks to CNN's Tom Johnson, Bob Furnad, and Jay Suber for listening to my ideas and giving me a chance.

My life on the road would not be nearly as snafu-free without the services of my trusty travel agent Jerry Powell of Century Travel in Atlanta. Only the *best* travel agents will survive in the coming years, and I'm sure Jerry will be one of them.

Living in Atlanta, it's impossible to cover business travel without running into Delta Air Lines, and I'd like to thank all the folks there who have helped me along. While it may seem that I pick on our hometown carrier, it's only out of an almost familial fondness. Delta is a good airline, full of a lot of great people. I'm lucky to have it in my backyard.

One of my more rewarding activities is covering the travel industry for Grassroots Research, a division of San Francisco-based Dresdner RCM Global Investors. Monitoring the financial side of the travel industry provides an important perspective. Thanks especially to Clare Tarushka, a truly global manager.

I'd also like to thank the various public relations professionals out there who have helped make my life easier by arranging those key interviews or providing that one little shred of information that can make or break a story. PR is one of the great unthanked professions, so here's a big *thank you*!

Finally, I'd like to thank Cynthia Zigmund, my editor in 1993, who tracked me down and got my first book, *202 Tips Even the Best Business Travelers May Not Know*, off the ground. I trust that the guidance she provided as my editor back then results in an even better book this time around.

Happy travels!

Christopher McGinnis
February 1998

THE UNOFFICIAL BUSINESS TRAVELER'S POCKET GUIDE

PART ONE

The Trip

CHAPTER 1

Things to Know Before You Go

1—STAY INSIDE THE INFORMATION LOOP

Among business travelers, the phrase "knowledge is power" rings truer than ever. While a basic understanding of this $160 billon market is important, sometimes it's the details that can make or break a business trip. How would you know to ask for an upgrade to first class if you didn't know it was even a possibility? How would you find out that a new non-stop flight to a well-traveled destination could shave a couple hours or dollars off your journey? How do you find out about that new hotel just around the corner from your client in Denver offering double miles in your favorite airline frequent flier program? Smart business travelers have learned to quickly sift through the mountain of news, offers, deals, and come-ons to find out what and who is *really* worth listening to.

Read up! Stay in tune with the travel industry. Aside from what you are holding in your hands, here are some of the best sources of business travel information.

- CNN covers business travel topics on its *Morning News* show ("Business Travel and Beyond"), on *Headline News,* and on its CNN Airport Network.
- The *Wall Street Journal*'s "Takeoffs & Landings Travel" column, which appears in the Friday Weekend Journal section, usually begins with a topical article on the front page and continues on a full page deeper in the section.
- In addition to the travel industry news reported in *USA Today*'s Money section, a special column (aptly called "Business Travel") appears every Tuesday. Also watch for *USA Today*'s business travel pullout sections, which appear every quarter.
- *The New York Times* runs a helpful "Business Travel" column every Wednesday in the Business Day section. The Sunday Travel section is also a good place to look. Although mostly devoted to leisure travel, you'll find periodic reporting on business travel topics. Especially helpful is a regular feature called "The Practical Traveler."
- The business sections of some smart local papers now carry local or syndicated columns addressing the business traveler. See the *Los Angeles Times*

"Executive Travel" column every Wednesday and the *Atlanta Journal-Constitution* "Business Traveler" and the *Philadelphia Inquirer* "Business Travel" columns every Monday.

- *Condé Nast Traveler* and *Travel and Leisure* magazines usually include at least one good business travel report in each issue.
- There's a plethora of helpful travel newsletters and magazines, but the best for business travelers include the Consumer Reports Travel Letter, which covers the industry with factual, objective, Naderesque zeal ($39/year, tel: 800-234-1970); *InsideFlyer* for frequent traveler program information ($36/year, tel: 800-767-8896); *Frequent Flyer,* which is usually sent along with the *Official Airline Guide* and provides good national and international coverage ($24/year, tel: 800-323-3537); *The Ticket,* which is mainly for business travelers based in the Southeast ($34/year, tel: 404-327-9696); and *Best Fares,* which helps travelers with back-to-back or hidden city fares and other travel deals ($49.95/year, tel: 800-635-3033). Hard-core information seekers should look into trade publications: *Business Travel News,* for corporate travel managers ($95/year, tel: 800-447-0138), or *Travel Weekly,* for travel agents ($29/year, tel: 800-360-0015). Call and ask for a trial issue, then decide whether or not to subscribe.

- Other sources include frequent flier program statements, travel agency newsletters, and the best source of all—other business travelers.

2—WORK THE WEB

The Internet and the World Wide Web are quickly becoming central sources of business travel information. The beauty of the Web is that information is instantaneous. It's the perfect medium for rapidly changing information that business travelers try to keep up with every day. And since business travelers are more likely to use the Internet than the general population, sites designed specially for them are sprouting up fast.

Browsing through the World Wide Web is like walking through a flea market—enticing, inviting, but frustrating and slow. Everyone is hawking something. And like a flea market, it can take many hours of scouting around to find just what applies to you. Listed below are a few good places to start—but because of the ever-changing nature of the Web, these sites could have changed, moved, or dissolved by the time you read this. The best way to get the information you need is to go to a search engine like www.excite.com or www.yahoo.com, and enter the words "business travelers" or "frequent fliers" plus your home town or destination, and see what pops up. Here are some more specific sites to check out.

- Business travel booking sites (on-line agencies) include www.thetrip.com and www.biztravel.com. These sites also include a heavy dose of practical editorial advice to help with just about every aspect of your trip. You'll also find useful destination information and links to other helpful sites.

- Other general travel booking sites are www.travelocity.com, www.expedia.com, www.itn.com, www.americanexpress. com, or www.previewtravel.com.
- For good late-breaking news, click on the travel button at www.usatoday.com, www.cnn.com, www.cnnfn.com, or www.msnbc.com.
- For links to all major airport and airline Web sites, see www.airlines-online.com.

3—GET USED TO BOOKING YOUR TRAVEL ON-LINE

The Web is mostly a place where business travelers go to gather information rather than book tickets, but that's changing fast. Experts estimate that revenue from on-line travel bookings will mushroom to $3.1 billion by the year 2000. Booking simple out-and-back trips (the bulk of business trips) is easy on most travel agency or airline Web sites. But if you need help with a multiple-leg or international trip, or the airline seat of your choice, or a hotel room with a view, it's good to know that a human travel agent is still around.

4—SIGN UP FOR SPECIAL ON-LINE DISCOUNTS

Airlines are constantly faced with the "brown banana" problem. Their unsold inventory "spoils" every time a plane takes off with empty seats. Enter the all-powerful World Wide Web—the ideal place to unload this potential spoilage. The tool: Internet-only sale fares and auctions. There are variations among airlines, but in general, the deeply discounted Internet-only fares (to cities of the airlines' choosing) are posted on airline sites or automatically e-mailed on Wednesday for flights departing the following Saturday and returning that Monday or Tuesday. These restrictions make it hard, if not impossible, for business travelers to use. But if you're looking for an inexpensive weekend getaway, you won't find a better deal anywhere. (See specific airline Web sites to sign up.)

5—SAY GOODBYE TO YOUR AIRLINE TICKET

Anyone who has made a hotel reservation should be familiar with the airlines' new electronic or "ticketless" option. You call the airline or your travel agent, order your ticket, provide your credit card number for payment, and get a confirmation number in return. When you get to the airport, you provide the confirmation number and/or personal identification, wait in line for your boarding pass, and get on the plane.

Ticketless air travel is a good thing because there is no longer a need to have to pick up a paper ticket from a city ticket office, travel agent, or airport check-in counter. You can simply call in your reservation and appear at the airport gate with your ID. You don't need a courier to deliver your ticket (or lose it), forcing you to pay extra for a "prepaid" ticket or a lost ticket (around $70).

The downside of ticketless travel? There's one more line to stand in to get your boarding pass. And there's less of a permanent record of the trip in order to back up claims for unposted frequent flier miles. Also, there are potential problems during unplanned events—like flight cancellations—when you must be booked on another carrier.

6—CHOOSE A GOOD TRAVEL AGENT

Do you think that travel agents lead glamorous lives, with some work, but mostly play? Do you think that they probably spend more time on warm beaches than at their desks? Think again. High pressure, high turnover, thin profit margins, cutthroat competition, complex technology, and a constantly changing product are the reality of the travel agency business. In almost all cases, it is wiser to use a trusted travel agent than to call travel suppliers directly. But how do you find a good travel agent?

- First, define the services you need from a travel agent; write them down.
- Determine fees. Recent cuts in the commissions that airlines pay travel agents mean that travelers now have to foot the bill for certain travel agency services. These fees vary depending on your travel volume and patterns—and they're negotiable.
- Ask around. Finding a good travel agent is like finding a good doctor or accountant. Use your network of business contacts, friends, or consultants for recommendations. When you find a good one, stick with him, and refer him to others.
- Meet the agency owners and managers. Be sure you are comfortable with them. Let them know that you are seeking a

long-term relationship. Meet the agents. How long have they been in the business? How familiar are they with your specific travel needs?

- Find out if the agency is biased toward certain air carriers. Some travel agencies earn overrides or percentage points that are added to the standard 8 percent commission the airlines pay only if they favor one airline (and can prove it). If that is the case, you may not always get the lowest fare. However, agencies with these "preferred" relationships are in a better position to pull strings with the airlines to get their clients out of travel jams—and even score upgrades.
- Ask about the specialty of the agency. Some agencies are better at leisure travel than business travel, although few will admit it. (You may not want to use a business travel agent to book your honeymoon in St. Lucia or a leisure travel agent to book your four-city sales junket.)
- Does the agency have an on-line booking site? If so, is it cheaper to book on-line than with a human agent?

7—MAKE PROPER AIRLINE RESERVATIONS

Airfares are confusing to even the most seasoned traveler. Some clarification is in order.

- The lowest fare available (discounted coach) is usually not used by business travelers because it requires an advance purchase of 14 to 21 days, a Saturday night stayover, charges $75 penalties for changes, and is nonrefundable.

- Most of the upstart, low-fare, or niche carriers, offer low unrestricted fares between a growing number of cities. Most do not require a Saturday night stayover; however, most require an advance purchase of 14 to 21 days for the cheapest seats.
- More expensive full-coach fares are a more popular option for midweek flying travelers. No Saturday night stay is required. There are no penalties for changes or refunds. Some airlines allow automatic upgrades to first class if flying on certain routes on full-coach fares.
- Minimally restricted business-class fares are only available on transcontinental or international flights.
- First-class fares carry the same minimal restrictions as full-coach fares. Members of airline frequent travel programs can sometimes ask for special discounts on first-class fares.

8—UNDERSTAND THE RULES FOR DISCOUNT FARES

To save money, some business travelers are forced to turn to more restricted discounted coach fares, which require a Saturday night stay. Rules for these tickets are confusing and vary considerably between airlines. Generally:

- Nonrefundable fares have a maximum stay of 30 days.
- The return flight can be changed for an airline-imposed fee (currently $75 on most major carriers), provided a discount seat is available.
- The outbound (first leg) flight can only be changed if the same fare is still offered and the advance purchase requirement is met. Again, the change fee will apply.
- If the same fare is not offered, ask for the best available nonrefundable fare and apply your original ticket toward it. You will then pay any fare difference, including the service fee.
- Partially used nonrefundable tickets generally have no refund value and cannot be applied toward another ticket.

9—KNOW THE AIRLINE'S LINE You've heard this tip before. In fact, anyone who travels on business hears it regularly. "Book as far in advance as possible to get the best airfare." Sound familiar? Unfortunately, that tip doesn't work for business travelers anymore. If you don't want to stay over a Saturday night (like any business traveler with a life), it doesn't matter if you book two weeks, a month, or three months ahead of time. Airfares that allow you to come home on weekends are stuck at higher levels than ever. Why are business airfares—those that do not require a Saturday night stayover or advance purchase *so* much more expensive than leisure fares? While it seems like an unfair situation, here's how the airlines explain it: Business travelers like convenience—meaning plenty of flights to choose from—and plenty of backup flights if plans change. Usually they can't make their plans very far in advance. High fares are a market-driven way to keep those valuable last-minute seats open. If they did not hold these seats at higher fare levels, the airlines claim that all their planes would be full of lower-fare leisure travelers, leaving no seats for business travelers.

10—CONSIDER LOW-FARE AIRLINES

This high-fare situation is alleviated somewhat in cities where low-fare carriers have a presence. Low-fare carriers rarely impose the onerous Saturday night stayover restriction that the major airlines do. As a matter of fact, in markets where low-fare carriers fly, the majors lift their Saturday night restrictions and offer at least a handful of seats that match low-fare carriers' cheap prices and lack of restrictions. But low-fare carriers only cover a small patch of the business travel landscape.

11—GET CREATIVE WITH TICKETING

Business travelers typically fly midweek and cannot take advantage of cheaper airfares that require a Saturday night stayover. Unfortunately, this forces the cost-conscious to bend the rules in order to find affordable fares. While the airlines consider this practice unethical—because they feel that you are being deceptive—some travelers opt for "creative" ticketing strategies to save money.

- A "back-to-back" fare works when (for a midweek trip) it is cheaper to buy two roundtrip tickets that require a Saturday night stay than one unrestricted, full-coach fare. "Back-to-backers" buy one round-trip ticket that starts in their hometown and another ticket that originates in their destination. Then they simply use the outbound portion of each ticket and throw away the second half. This may be much cheaper than one unrestricted full-coach fare—savings can be as much as 50 percent.
- A "hidden-city" fare is created when competing air carriers are forced to meet fare pricing set by a competitor within a certain market. In doing so, carriers will sometimes offer a lower fare to a destination that connects through one of their higher-priced hub cities. To take advantage of hidden-city fares, book your flight to the least expensive city (beyond your final destination) and simply get off when the plane stops at the higher-priced hub city. These work best when buying one-way fares. *Warning:* Carry on all your luggage so that it isn't sent to the ticketed destination.

If you're having difficulty understanding these arcane measures, just ask your travel agent how they work. Some travel agents are more than happy to privately oblige; others refuse. Ask around. But beware: The airlines are trying to track down offenders, charging full fare at the gate and even threatening to take away frequent flier privileges.

12—CONSIDER ALTERNATE AIRPORTS

Another way to get around high fares and tight restrictions is by flying to nearby airports. Most major business travel destinations have a smaller secondary airport that usually handles low-fare or regional flights. Many times a major carrier will match fares and lower restrictions to both the primary and secondary airports. The key is that you must *ask* your travel agent to check for fares to these secondary airports. Some examples:

- *Los Angeles:* The LA basin boasts four airports in addition to Los Angeles International (LAX). These include Long Beach, Orange County, Ontario, and Burbank.
- *Chicago:* O'Hare is the major airport, but many large carriers will match the low fares that the smaller carriers offer to nearby Midway Airport. With the recent introduction of an El (metro) stop, many travelers prefer Midway to the sprawling and crowded O'Hare. Low-fare seekers may also consider flying to nearby Milwaukee—about an hour north of Chicago.
- *Washington D.C.:* Ronald Reagan National is the city's close-in convenient airport, but also the most expensive. Suburban Dulles International and nearby Baltimore/Washington International offer much better deals.
- *San Francisco:* Considering traffic, it is sometimes faster to drive across the bay bridge from Oakland Airport than to

drive up the peninsula from San Francisco International. Those willing to drive a bit further may find a lower fare at San Jose or Sacramento airports.

- Other primary-secondary airport examples: Miami and Ft. Lauderdale; Denver and Colorado Springs; Houston Intercontinental and Houston Hobby; Dallas/Ft. Worth International and Dallas Love Field. And fares in and out of Newark are usually somewhat cheaper than New York's La Guardia or Kennedy airports.

13—USE YOUR FREQUENT FLIER MILES TO "BUY" HIGH-PRICED TICKETS

Using your frequent flier miles to get around high fares is getting more difficult. For example, Continental now requires a Saturday night stayover when redeeming the basic 25,000-mile reward for a free round trip. If you want to travel in midweek or during a "blackout" period, you'll have to redeem closer to 40,000 miles. With frequent flier miles roughly valued at about 2 cents each, it only makes sense to redeem 40,000 miles if the fare you would otherwise pay exceeds about $800.

14—KNOW YOUR CODE

Be aware of the airline trend toward a relatively new phenomenon called *code sharing,* in which more than one airline sells seats on the same flight. (One flight "shares" several airline "codes," so although your ticket says DL for Delta, the plane you fly on says Swissair or SR.) One important detail about code sharing: With more than one airline selling seats on a flight, you may be able to find cheaper seats if you shop among partners. One airline won't quote you the price being asked by its partner, even if it's for the very same flight. A good travel agent should tell you, however. While it is confusing, code sharing benefits frequent flier program members because it expands earning and redemption opportunities.

15—BEWARE OF FEES

International travelers should be wary of "departure fees" usually required as you clear customs on your way out of the country. Many countries require that the payment (sometimes hefty) be made in cash at the airport. In the United States, the steep $24 fee is added to the cost of your airline ticket.

16—KNOW THE DIFFERENCE BETWEEN A DEBIT CARD AND A CREDIT OR CHARGE CARD

When it comes to business travel, it's important to know the difference between a debit card and a credit or charge card. Debit and credit cards look very similar; both carry the recognizable MasterCard and Visa logos. But be sure you know which is which when you pull them out of your wallet on the road.

A debit card charge is immediately withdrawn from your checking account—just like an ATM transaction. When you purchase an airline ticket with a debit card, the funds come out of your account instantly, but they cannot be instantly refunded if you change your mind. Many car rental companies and hotels will only accept debit cards as final payment. To check out a car, or check in the hotel, you need a credit card.

Therefore, it's smart to keep your travel purchases on standard credit or charge cards. In addition, MasterCard, Visa, American Express, and Diners Club credit cards offer protection from airline bankruptcy, as well as car rental and life insurance benefits. Even more important, debit card purchases don't earn frequent flier miles like the many affinity credit cards do.

17—USE AIRLINE ON-TIME PERFORMANCE DATA

Most surveys indicate that business travelers' top concern regarding air travel is on-time performance. The Department of Transportation tracks the airlines in this regard and publishes statistics in its monthly *Air Travel Consumer Report* (www.dot.gov).

You can actually ask for the on-time performance of any flight when you make your reservation. Most travelers don't know about this, but the on-time performance for individual flights is tracked monthly on all reservations systems. When making your reservation, ask the agent for the on-time performance of the flight, and you will be given a score for the flight on a scale of 1 to 9, with 1 meaning that the flight was on time between 1 and 10 percent of the time, and 9 meaning that the flight was on time 90 to 100 percent of the time in the preceding month. The airlines do not openly publicize this, so few people ever inquire. Always ask if being on time is crucial in your decision. (These scores are also usually listed with on-line booking sites.)

18—TRADE SHOW TIPS Watch out for huge trade shows or sporting events that can clog a city's airport and fill hotels unexpectedly. But if you are headed to that crowded show, here are some survival tips.

- Opt for *preregistration,* if possible, to avoid long lines at on-site registration. For a high-tech twist, many large conventions now allow preregistration via special Web pages.
- Set up meetings with important contacts *before* the convention, because once you get there, you'll be competing with hundreds of other attendees, not to mention cocktail parties, banquets, and breakout meetings.
- While trade shows are a big part of doing business in the United States, the concept is even more popular overseas. No smoking, no eating rules that are standard at U.S. trade shows may not apply elsewhere. Europeans use trade shows as an opportunity to do business, like signing major contracts or making deals, whereas Americans tend to use trade shows for networking and relationship maintenance.
- Bring your cell phone, or rent one on-site. During breaks or before or after meals, convention center phone banks are packed. A good idea: Many hotels and car rental companies will rent

business travelers cell phones for the duration of their stay.

- Forget about that new pair of Kenneth Cole shoes you've been wanting to show off to all your colleagues. Stick with a nice-looking but comfortably broken-in pair. Women should avoid heels—not just because they can be uncomfortable when worn for long periods, but because trade show floors are usually uneven and full of obstacles like carpet wrinkles and electrical wiring.
- If you plan on collecting lots of brochures, premiums, and other goodies at the trade show, consider using a backpack or external luggage dolly to drag your cache behind you. Carrying around a heavy bag for hours is hard on your hands, arms, and lower back. To avoid the hassle of carrying your stash back home with you, simply ship the material to your office. Many smart overnight mail companies have set up shop on trade show floors for this purpose.
- Another timeworn, but essential piece of advice: Don't forget those follow-up notes to important clients or new prospects. Write them while you are at the convention, or on the plane home.

19—KNOW HOW TO USE BUSINESS CARDS

How many times have you heard people say, "Bring lots of business cards"? It's true, a business card is an essential tool at any large meeting. Here are some other tips for using them.

- Stay organized. Reserve one pocket for "inbound" cards from new contacts. Upon getting a new card, write a few words describing the nature of your meeting on the back. This will prove helpful when writing your follow-up notes.
- Reserve another pocket for "outbound" cards—your own. Never mix inbound and outbound cards. It looks unprofessional to fish through a stack of other cards for one of your own.
- Tip for women: Many business suits have few or no pockets. In this case, use your plastic name-badge holder as a card holder: keep a supply of your business cards tucked behind the badge.
- If you travel frequently to the same country or region, have your business information printed in its predominant language on the reverse side of your card.

20—DON'T FORGET ABOUT FIDO AND FLUFFY

Have you run out of friends or neighbors willing to take care of your pet when you are traveling on business? It might be time to look into hiring a professional pet sitter. The key to doing this is to hire a service that is licensed, bonded, and insured. There are a growing number of professional pet sitters throughout the United States; many are members of an organization called the National Association of Professional Pet Sitters (NAPPS). Each company provides different services: feeding one or two times a day, dog walking, cat and dog bathing or grooming, cleaning litter boxes, administering medications, or taking your pet to the veterinarian. They'll even provide "theft-deterrent" services like picking up newspapers or turning lights on and off. Call NAPPS at 1-800-296-PETS, or see www.petsitters.org.

21—SOME FINAL PRETRIP TIPS

- Always write down your hotel and car rental confirmation numbers on your airline ticket jacket or in your daily organizer. These numbers are vital if your reservation is lost, the computers are down, or you are denied your room or car. When getting your confirmation number, ask for your reservationist's name. The reservationist will be more likely to make sure that all parts of your reservation are correct if she knows her name is attached to it.
- To get the lowest rate, you must ask for it two or three times throughout the reservation process. Reservationists are trained not to give away the store if they don't have to, so be sure to *ask*. "Is this the lowest rate available?" "Are there any specials on now?" "Can I get a better deal?" "Is the corporate rate the lowest rate?" "What other cheaper rates are available?" "What would I have to do to qualify for the cheapest rate?" Check airfares before you depart. Has a low-cost carrier recently added flights to your destination, and brought down fares across the board? Shop around at the car rental counters for the best rate;

use your reservation only if you can't find a better deal.

- Write all your frequent traveler program numbers and frequently called 800 numbers on a pocket-sized piece of paper for easy access.
- Always have your travel agent or reservationist provide you with a seat assignment and your boarding pass before you get to the airport. *Note:* In early 1998, some airlines stopped issuing advance boarding passes. Now that you must show photo ID at the gate agent anyway, an advance boarding pass is little more than a security blanket. But you should still request your seat assignment ahead of time.
- A *nonstop flight* means just that—no stops. A *direct flight* means that the plane will stop at least once before reaching its final destination. Know the difference.

Confessions of a Frequent Traveler: Cleveland

It seems that everyone (except business travelers) thinks that our lifestyle—or rather, our workstyle—is "glamorous." All they see are doting flight attendants bearing pillows and caviar, luxurious hotel rooms, limousine transfers, and glitzy expense account–paid restaurant meals. Most readers of this book should know all about that myth.

I was reminded of reality on a less-than-glam business trip to Cleveland to attend the National Business Travel Association's annual convention.

After a screeching, last-minute arrival at my airport gate on Sunday night, I discovered that my flight was on Air Traffic Control hold because of a storm in Cleveland. Once I boarded the plane and got situated in my exit-row window seat, a family of four appeared bearing boarding cards with my seat number on them. They all wanted to sit together, so the flight attendant asked me to wait at the back of the plane while he found me a new seat. He finally found one—a center seat at the back of the plane. (And I was hoping for one of those occasional upgrades to first class!)

We arrived in Cleveland around 10 P.M. I'm a big fan of on-airport rapid rail connections, and I knew Cleveland had a train stop, but found that it took a while, as Hopkins Airport was under renovation and most directional signs were down.

After a few wrong turns, I found the entrance, made my way down a long, hot corridor to the tracks, and waited . . . and waited . . . and waited. Then I realized that no one else was waiting with me. So I walked back to the entrance and saw a small sheet of paper taped to the entryway informing me that owing to construction, trains did not operate after 10 P.M. A city bus that followed the route of the train would leave at 10:35 from the upper-level roadway. A city bus? Never, I thought, as I decided to throw the budget to the wind and take a cab.

As I exited the ground transportation area, another thunderstorm was wreaking havoc with the masses streaming to rental car shuttles, parking lots, and private cars. I saw no cabs. I asked a security guard where the taxi stand was, and he pointed to the other end of the airport. So I hoofed it down there, only to find 30 or so hot, wet, frustrated unglamorous business travelers waiting for the occasional cab to enter the airport.

So I switched to plan C—that city bus. I went back to the upper level and found the bus stop populated by that night's airport cleaning crew. We all sat on a Southwest Airlines luggage cart, lamely looking out at the tremendous electrical storm in the distance: they with their tattered shopping bags and umbrellas, me with my briefcase and hang-up bag. After a 15-minute conversation that ranged from where I was from and what I was doing, to sore feet, the heat wave, and the difference between *Atlanta* and *Atlantic City*, the bus arrived.

After a 20-minute ride, we arrived at my stop. I dashed across a giant parking lot through the drizzle to my hotel—a Budgetel, one of the only hotels in town that still had rooms when I finally decided to attend the conference the week before.

Anyway, I dashed into the lobby, hot, wet, and bothered only to find another paper sign taped to the check-in counter asking guests to register in the hotel office around the corner and down the hall.

There I found a frazzled but friendly duo registering guests by hand—writing names and room numbers on a long sheet of paper, then handing out keys. Seems that the hotel had been struck by lightning that evening. The power was back on, but the phones and other electronic gadgetry were still out. Hence the manual check-in—and oh yes, the manual wake-up call the next morning (a knock on the door). Who said business travel was glamorous?

CHAPTER 2

What to Bring and How to Bring It

Frequent travel is as tough on bags as it is on travelers. Proper packing and lugging can help make a business trip easy. Pack too much and you'll strain your body, wrinkle your clothes, and run into delays with skycaps and porters or at baggage claim. Choose the wrong type of luggage and it will turn into a ball and chain. Read on for tips that will help keep you light on your feet and looking good.

22—CHOOSE THE BEST LUGGAGE

- Don't sacrifice strength and durability for price. Look for bags with durable stitching and zippers, metal buckles, and padded handles or shoulder straps. If you can afford leather, buy it. Otherwise, look for heavy-duty "ballistic" nylon, or nylon and leather combinations. Color? When in doubt, opt for black—it doesn't show scuffs and always looks good. However, black bags are more difficult to identify on the luggage carousel. Make yours unique by tying on a bright piece of yarn or dabbing on a spot of bright paint.

- Many business travelers are now opting for soft briefcases rather than the traditional hard-sided attachés. Laptops fit more comfortably into the top-opening, soft-sided models, and they stow more easily on the plane. In choosing a soft-sided case, look for *full-grain* leather as opposed to less expensive leather grains. The investment will pay off in durability and appearance.
- "Wheels" were once used almost universally by flight attendants—the ultimate road warriors. But more and more business travelers are trying out wheeled luggage these days. These carry-on-sized suitcases are typically made of durable nylon with built-in wheels and an extension handle that adjusts to the traveler's height. The telescoping handle should feel sturdy and lock into place when extended. Also look for wheels that are as big and as far apart as possible. This will make the suitcase easy to maneuver and keep it from tipping over.
- New airline rules limit liability for any handles or wheels that are broken when wheeled suitcases are checked in. If possible, always carry on your wheels and check larger suitcases.

- Remember, personal luggage tags are easily shorn from bags. Be sure that you have proper identification inside as well as outside your bag. And remove all old airline-issued claim tags, or your checked baggage may end up at the wrong destination.
- Did you know that if you use your luggage exclusively for business travel, you can write it off as a business expense? So go ahead and splurge a little. You'll be glad you did.

23—CHOOSE THE BEST CLOTHING

- The key word is black. It is classic and works well in almost every situation. Just don't forget your lint brush.
- Bring clothes that you can mix and match. If embarking on a longer, two- or three-suit trip, try to bring all outfits with the same general color scheme. Blacks, grays, and khakis work well. Don't bring anything that you can't mix and match.
- Although hotel valet and laundry services are expensive, they're well worth it if you don't haul around more clothes than you need.
- These days, business travelers have two options when it comes to raincoats: the traditional water-repellent, all-cotton, trench coat styles or the new and increasingly popular anorak styles made of polyester microfiber. Microfiber coats are more water-repellent and lighter and they

don't wrinkle. London Fog's "Packable Traveler" line runs from $119 to $129.

24—AVOID WRINKLES

- Wool or cotton-polyester blends do not wrinkle as much as pure wool or 100 percent cotton. Don't even think about traveling with linen, which wrinkles at the sight of a suitcase.
- Pack clothes in the plastic bags from the dry cleaners, which prevent wrinkles by allowing clothes in your suitcase to slide instead of rubbing up against each other.
- Hang wrinkled clothes in the bathroom and close the door during your shower. Wrinkles will fall out.
- Most hotels will supply an iron and ironing board on request.
- Pack larger items first, then stuff rolled-up underwear, socks, or other items around them.

25—TOILET KIT SUGGESTIONS

If you are a regular traveler, have a toilet kit permanently packed with your usual items for use on the road only. This keeps you from having to reassemble your kit each time you take a trip.

Buy a set of small, plastic, travel-sized bottles (available at many drugstores) for packing your potions and lotions. Don't fill them to the top as changes in aircraft cabin pressure cause leaks. Pack all liquids that might leak together in a resealable bag. Be sure aerosols (shaving cream, mousse, hairspray) have their plastic protective tops attached.

Always pack your toilet kit in your carry-on bag. You never know what might happen to a bag in the belly of the plane. Otherwise, keep a bottle filled with aspirin or any prescription drugs you might lose, and store it in your carry-on bag. (The same goes for contact lens solution and a lens storage case.)

26—LITTLE THINGS COUNT

- Pack shoes in plastic bags to avoid soiling your clothes. (Use the ones supplied by hotel laundry services.)
- Two axioms to remember: "If you have to check it, don't bring it," and "Bring half as many clothes and twice as much money."
- Keep a roll of Scotch tape in your bag at all times. It can be used to quickly mend hems, seal bottles, or remove lint from those black outfits. Also, carry a prepacked travel sewing kit that includes a needle, thread, and a few buttons.
- If you are in a mad rush for the airport, don't fret about whether or not you have packed everything you could conceivably need. Remember that you can buy just about anything you may need at your destination.
- If there's no way you can carry on a valuable item, consider purchasing excess valuation insurance when you check your bags. It costs about $1 per $100 in declared value.

- Remove or secure the hook on your hang-up bag or any other handle or appendage that could get caught or snagged in the airline baggage-handling systems.

27—COPING WITH CARRY-ONS

Recently, the airlines have gone to great lengths to lay the blame on *passengers* for carrying on too many bags. But why is it that travelers opt to carry on the majority of their luggage? Is it because they want to inconvenience airline employees? Hardly. Passengers have a well-founded distrust of the airlines' baggage-handling system. Most seasoned travelers have had a bag delayed, lost, pilfered, or destroyed at one time or another.

Over the last decade, the airlines have crammed as many seats as possible into each plane, removing any hint of legroom. Many have gone so far as to remove closets and shelves that were once used to handle overflow from overhead bins in order to install extra seats. And passenger loads are at an all-time high. That means there is precious little space for *any* carry-on.

- If you must carry on a larger-than-average bag, get on the plane as early as possible. Overhead bins fill up fast—particularly during the cold winter months and the holidays.
- If you bring more than two carry-ons (the "official" limit on many carriers), put one bag inside another. Gate agents usually scrutinize the number of bags rather than bag dimensions. Typical

airline dimensions allow one bag no larger than 9 x 14 x 22 inches (can fit under seat) and another bag 10 x 14 x 36 inches (can fit in overhead bin) or a garment bag 4 x 23 x 45 inches (can fit in closet). *Note:* A briefcase is considered a piece of carry-on luggage, while a woman's purse may not be.

- At the end of 1997, some airlines adopted a "1 plus" rule regarding carry-on bags, meaning that you are allowed one carry-on, plus a briefcase, purse, or laptop. Airlines are battling to reach a general consensus as to the number of carry-on bags each passenger is permitted. However, until an across-the-board decree is dispatched by the Federal Aviation Administration, the issue will remain frustratingly vague and unresolved.
- Pack your bags with the possibility of having to check them in mind. With airlines and flight attendants scrutinizing carry-ons more than ever, you may be forced to gate-check your bag. In that case, be sure that your valuables and any electronic gear are in the bag you carry on the plane. The best part about gate checking is that bags are usually waiting by the plane door as you exit—not at the delay-prone baggage carousel. However, this is not always the case: always ask if your gate-checked bag will be waiting for you as you exit the plane or in the baggage claim area.

28—PLAN MORE AND LUG LESS

- If you're traveling by car, pack a smaller bag for hotel and motel stops en route. This way you don't have to lug *all* your heavy bags into every hotel or motel on the way. *Important:* Be sure that the bags you do leave in your car are out of sight. Use your judgment in deciding whether it is smart to leave anything in the car overnight.
- If you are assigned to a certain city on an ongoing Monday through Friday schedule, you might tire of hauling your bags back and forth between your home and the same hotel every week. Inquire about leaving your bags at the hotel. Many "business" hotels are virtually empty on weekends. Inquire about the possibility of simply leaving your clothes in your room without charge.

29—LAPTOP LUGGING

It's estimated that business travelers buy about 5 million new laptop or notebook computers each year. If you are considering buying a notebook or upgrading to a newer model, your main consideration should be *weight.* Notebooks are getting lighter and more powerful all the time. For example, many new top-of-the-line models pack a floppy as well as a CD-ROM disk drive, a big 12-inch color screen, a 4-hour battery, stereo speakers, a built-in AC adapter, and a standard keyboard in a neat 6- to 7-pound notebook-sized box. But do you really need all that? If you are willing to give up things like floppy or CD drives and full-size keyboards, some sub-notebooks can weigh as little as 4 pounds.

Battery life is about to reach transcontinental flight limits. Most new units using newer lithium ion batteries last up to four hours. Older nickel metal-hydride batteries can last anywhere from two to four hours. By the time this book is published there will be even longer-lasting batteries—and electrical plug-ins on planes should become more common.

The near ubiquity of public PC kiosks with Web browsers (in hotels, airports, and convention centers) and new Web-based e-mail means that those who use laptops as little more than communications devices may be able to leave them at home.

TEN WAYS TO KNOW YOU HAVE TOO MANY CARRY-ONS

According to Southwest Airlines, you know you have too many carry-ons when . . .

1. Other customers keep asking, "So, where are you moving?"
2. It takes you longer to load you bags than it would to charter your own airplane.
3. You actually packed the kitchen sink.
4. You need two cars to get to the airport.
5. Your carry-on bags are bigger than you are.
6. You are told your carry-ons alone exceed the baggage weight for the entire plane.

7. You can't walk down the aisle without knocking out other passengers.
8. Your luggage takes up the entire side of the plane.
9. You have more bags than arms.
10. It takes you longer to get your bags off the plane than it does for checked luggage to arrive at baggage claim.

CHAPTER 3

Getting to and from the Airport

Every journey begins with a single step, so the saying goes. Well, almost every business trip begins and ends with a single trip to and from the airport. And the trip between the airport and your meeting or your home could be more involved and arduous than a 2000-mile journey across the country.

Has this ever happened to you?

Your 5 P.M. flight has landed and you've retrieved your bags. Now you want to get into town and your hotel is only guaranteed until 6 P.M. What's the best way? How much will a cab cost? Is there an airport limousine or van? How often? How long does it take? Is there a rapid rail link that could beat traffic?

Or . . .

Your meeting has just ended and your flight home leaves in an hour. You are in a strange city and you have to pick the fastest way to get to the airport. What do you do?

Airport transit choices are many and sometimes confusing. Speed, comfort, and cost are all factors in your choice. The key is to find the way that combines all three.

30—GETTING TO THE CITY

- Do not take the first conveyance you see as you exit the terminal—usually a taxicab—unless you know that is exactly what you need. Other factors to consider: Are you on a tight budget? Do you have too much luggage for the subway? Are you in a party of two or more? Do you need to recover your mental resources in the comfort of a limousine before a big meeting? Are you in the city for the first time?
- Travel agents can usually tell you in advance the various means of transportation available from the airport to your destination in the city or outlying communities.
- In larger cities, the airport authority usually operates a local or ground transportation desk near the baggage claim area to assist travelers in making frugal, intelligent, and safe choices. Don't accept rides from anyone who approaches you in the terminal unless you have already made prior arrangements.

31—BY TAXI

In most major cities you can just walk out of the airport or onto the curb and hail a cab. In smaller towns, beware—or plan ahead. There may not be enough taxis, and getting one could mean a long wait, especially if your flight arrives at an off-peak hour. Plan on waiting even longer if it is rainy or cold.

Most taxis have a laundry list of extra fees that you need to be wary of. Surcharges for ordering a cab by phone, per piece of luggage, airport pickup, time of day, and additional passengers seem to be at the driver's discretion. It is best to ask how much your ride will cost *before the trip begins,* even if there is a meter. Better yet, ask a friend or hotel concierge for a ballpark figure for how much you should spend on a cab to the airport. If you feel gypped, ask for a receipt with the driver's name and meter number on it.

32—BY CAR SERVICES

Sometimes limo companies offer car services—a sedan-sized version of their usual stretch offering, also known as "black-car service." Car services are most prevalent in New York City, but they are spreading to other cities. They represent a good value because they set a flat fee. Unexpected traffic delays can sometimes hike cab fares, which are usually based on an equation of distance traveled and time.

In 1997, car service companies in New York City (listed below) charged a variety of different fees for a car. Depending on the stature of the company, the make and model of the car, and the time of year you plan to rent, prices range between $20 and $110 for a trip between the airport and the city. All of the companies listed charge their fee, plus standard $3 to $5 tolls. (Remember that we are talking about New York City here, so don't forget to tip the driver.)

To book a car service, ask your travel agent, or call from home before you leave. Here's a list of some good New York City car services.

- Carey Limousine: 212-599-1122 (most expensive)
- Absolute: 800-ABSOLUT
- Big Apple: 800-692-3462
- Tel Aviv: 212-777-7777 (least expensive)

33—BY RAIL, SUBWAY, OR TRAIN

Rail connections are by far the most economical and fastest way to go, especially during roadway rush hours. Rapid rail service is inside, or a very close walk or shuttle ride from, airports in Atlanta, Boston, Chicago, Cleveland, Oakland, Philadelphia, St. Louis, and Washington, D.C. In the future, airports in San Francisco, Los Angeles, and other locations may also offer this service.

Rapid rail costs vary from city to city:

Atlanta	$1.50
Boston	$0.85
Chicago	$1.50
Cleveland	$1.50
Oakland	$2.00
Philadelphia	$5.00 to $6.00
St. Louis	$1.00
Washington, D.C.	$1.65

34—BY BUS OR VAN

Super Shuttle's trademark blue-and-yellow buses service 15 major airports across the United States and will provide transportation from home to airport or from airport to home, office, or hotel 24 hours a day, 7 days a week—all at a reasonable price. Call 800-258-3826 to make reservations, or visit them on-line at www.supershuttle.com.

Also, the blue Airporter (or similar) vans operating in many major cities take passengers wherever they want to go in a specific area, for a fraction of what a cab would cost. The downside is that you must sometimes wait while other passengers are picked up or dropped off. Ask about these services at the airport ground transportation desk.

Privately operated shuttle bus services, like the Carey Airport Express, Olympia Trails, or Gray Line bus services from the New York City airports, offer an excellent alternative to high-priced cabs.

Going from airport to city by municipally operated bus is really not a viable option for most business travelers. However, if you are a hardcore penny pincher, inquire at the airport ground transportation counter.

35—BY HOTEL SHUTTLE

Many business travelers forget to ask about this (usually) free service when making their reservations and end up paying exorbitant cab fares when they could have gone for free. Actually, courtesy airport shuttle services are built into your hotel rate, so if you don't use them you are actually paying twice. In many cities around the world travelers will find a bank of courtesy phones near the baggage claim area at the airport. It is wise to check there first to see if your hotel provides free shuttle service.

36—FAMILY MEMBERS If someone picks you up regularly at the airport, always have a designated pickup area in case all else fails. Having a regular backup meeting spot helps avoid the problems associated with flight delays, traffic delays, and miscommunication.

37—ON- OR OFF-AIRPORT PARKING If you decide to forgo public transportation to the airport because you would rather drive and park yourself, it pays to know all your options. Most on-airport lots are run by municipal governments and offer the basics—a close-in parking space—but not much else.

If you'd like to add bells and whistles to your parking experience, try the new breed of off-airport lot springing up on the perimeter of airports across the country. To entice customers away from on-airport lots, these small businesses offer frequent parker programs, car washes, tune-ups, laundry service, and other creative extras.

The best part about off-airport lots is that most have shuttles that follow you to your parking space, pick you (and your bags) up, and drop you off at the front door of the airport—no schlepping bags through a large, dark—or worse, rainy—parking lot. And most offer corporate programs for high-volume customers.

Another option: many airport hotels and car rental companies provide parking not only for usual customers, but for local parkers as well. (For more detailed discussion of car rentals, see Chapter 6, "On the Road.")

38—FIND A HELPFUL RESOURCE Travel agents, corporate travel managers, and travelers rely on Salk International's *Airport Transit Guide,* a complete guide to airport transfers at more than 400 airports around the world. The pocket-sized guide, revised each October, provides taxi rates, airport coach, limousine, car service, and van fares and schedules, public transit fares, schedules and routes, airport parking rates, car rental facilities, and helicopter services. Typically, travel agents, airlines, or hotels give the guide to their clients as premiums, but they can be ordered directly for $9.95 from Salk International Travel Premiums, Inc., PO Box 1388, Sunset Beach, CA 90742; tel. 800-962-4943; Web: www.io.com/salk. Here are some pearls of wisdom from the guide.

U.S. Cities

- To further simplify the process of getting to and from the airport, **Los Angeles** International Airport (LAX) has installed QuickAid, an automated information system, located in the baggage claim area and outside, near the exit. This computerized service offers schedules and fares for various forms of transportation. You can access QuickAid ahead of time by calling 310-646-5252. The system works well in an airport that can sometimes be confusing and chaotic.

(Estimated cab fare, LAX to downtown: $27 to $30.)

- For about $10, coaches called Airporters will bus you from **San Francisco**'s International Airport (SFO) to most hotels in the area. The coaches leave every half-hour and cost about a third as much as taking a taxi. In addition, SFO has an automated system of computer terminals located throughout the airport, where you can access information about transportation. (Estimated cab fare, SFO to downtown: $29.)
- At **Boston Logan** Airport (BOS), try the airport water shuttle. A free van leaves every 5 to 10 minutes from the airport to the water shuttle, which ferries passengers to Rowes Wharf, just next to the Boston Harbor Hotel. The boat leaves every 15 minutes, costs $8, and takes 7 minutes to cross the harbor. (Estimated cab fare, BOS to downtown: $15 to $25.)
- Delta offers water shuttle service from **New York**'s La Guardia Airport (LGA) to Manhattan. The free Delta shuttle bus departs the terminal every 15 minutes to the boat dock at the Marine Air Terminal. From there it is a 40-minute ride to Pier 11, at the corner of Wall and South streets, with an intermediate stop at 14th Street and the East River. Costs range from $15 to $25. (Estimated cab fare, LGA to Manhattan: $20.)
- At O'Hare Airport (ORD), a moving sidewalk transports you to the entrance of **Chicago**'s subway/elevated train

system, where for only $1.50 you are transported to the Loop in under 40 minutes. Some cars have baggage space. This trip is not advisable during peak rush hours, when cars are extremely crowded with locals, but otherwise it's an economical and efficient transfer. (Estimated cab fare, ORD to downtown: $30.)

International Cities

- Most hotels in London have stopped providing shuttle services to and from local airports. Instead, **London**'s Heathrow Airport (LHR) now offers a service called Hotel Hoppa, which departs every 10 to 15 minutes. For about $3.50, the buses will pick you up at the airport and transfer you to your hotel. Be sure to ask about discounts for senior citizens, military officials, and children and inquire about prepaid coupons and round-trip fares. Share taxis are also available and are marked as such—passengers riding in these cabs pay only a percentage of the total fare. In addition, a 15-minute high-speed train now runs from Heathrow to Paddington Station near Hyde Park. (Estimated cab fare, LHR to central London: $58.)
- At **London**'s Gatwick Airport (LGW), the Gatwick express train takes you into London for about $15, departing for Victoria Station every 15 minutes. Flightline buses will also transport you

for around $13, and they offer wide aisles, baggage space, and inside doors. The coaches leave hourly, and the ride lasts about 30 minutes; however, you must hail a cab from Victoria Station. (Estimated cab fare, Gatwick to the city: $66 to $82.)

- At **Tokyo**'s Narita Airport (NRT), now called New Tokyo International, a 60- to 90-minute cab ride will cost over $180! Instead, take the Skyliner Express, a 60-minute train that costs about $18.
- From **Munich**'s Munich Airport (MUC), the S-Bahn train #8 travels the 17.5 miles into this bustling Bavarian city in 40 to 45 minutes for about $9.50. (Estimated cab fare, MUC to central Munich: $51.)
- In **Paris**, the Air France coach system is continually improving; it provides excellent service to many points, and even offers special prices for three or four people. (You don't have to travel Air France in order to use this service, but as a bonus, the journey is free for Air France fliers.) From Charles de Gaulle Airport (CDG), the coach leaves every 12 minutes, and the 40-minute ride costs only around $10. The same service is available from Orly Airport (ORY) for about $15, with coaches departing every 20 minutes on a 60-minute ride. Paris continues to add new transfer services by bus, train, and limousine; however, Salk recommends the Air France coach system over other modes. (Estimated cab

fare to central Paris from CDG: $41; from ORY: $28.)

- In **Frankfurt** (FRA), Lufthansa has a masterful system of buses and trains that speed business travelers to many points throughout the country. The train segments carry flight numbers and are prebooked with your airline ticket. Lufthansa passengers pay nothing extra for the rail segments and have the option of taking the train or a Lufthansa flight segment. Business travel veterans almost always recommend the train. It is first class—with food, drink, and "flight attendants." Air traffic congestion combined with faster, more efficient trains may soon render much intra-European air travel obsolete. The train also operates from Stuttgart Airport four times per day. (Estimated cab fare, FRA to central Frankfurt: $25.)
- Be careful when hailing a cab at **Mexico City** Airport (MEX): the local government warns travelers to "use only authorized [cab] services. Use of any other service is on your own responsibility." Apparently, naïve travelers have been known to pay as much as double the fare when using an unauthorized cab service. Not only that, but the U.S. Embassy has issued warnings that robbery and assault can occur when hailing cruising or unofficial cabs. To avoid being taken advantage of by an unauthorized taxi service, look for the official ground transport signs in the arrival area at the airport. Government-

authorized cabs are white and mustard in color, and up to four people can ride for the price of one. (Estimated cab fare, MEX to downtown: $7.)

- Kingsford-Smith Airport (SYD) in **Sydney**, Australia, offers a convenient and cost-efficient service for travelers looking to get from the airport to their hotels. For about $4.50, the Kingsford-Smith bus stops at all hotels in Sydney. The alternate but not so appealing choice, the Airport Express, drops off at a central point in the city and costs almost $4, saving you less than $1. A new rail line should link the airport to the city in time for the 2000 Summer Olympic games. (Estimated cab fare, SYD to the central business district: $14.)
- Use caution when hailing a cab in **Warsaw**, **Budapest**, **Moscow**, or **Prague**. Apparently, cab drivers in these cities are known to engage in illegal practices; in other words, unauthorized cabs are likely to cost twice as much as an authorized taxi service. To avoid being swindled, use only authorized services in these areas, take a cab only where a dispatcher is present, and confirm fares before embarking. If possible, arrange for the hotel to send for a taxi.

Confessions of a Frequent Traveler: New York City

There's nothing better than a really good business trip to New York City. And nothing worse than a really bad one. In December 1997 I was lucky enough to experience one of the former.

Every December I have to be in New York for a few days to meet with my editors and publishers at *Fortune Magazine.* It's always a bit of a challenge because this is the busiest time of year in Manhattan, and hotels and flights are always hard to come by, especially on short notice.

As usual, the *Fortune* folks called around Thanksgiving and asked if I could meet on December 12. I was able to get a decent airfare from Atlanta ($345 round trip) because I was willing to stay over a Saturday night.

Finding a hotel was a different story. I asked my travel agent, searched the Web, and even called a few hotels directly—all sold out. In the end, I was able to snag a room that *Fortune* has on year-round reserve at the Surrey Hotel at $245 per night.

The flight up was, as usual, packed to the gills. Luckily, my briefcase and small suitcase fit in the overhead bin. Those that boarded late had to gate-check their bags. All they were allowed to carry on were coats and Sky Deli snacks.

Arrival at Newark was fine. This time I had booked a car service to get me from the airport to Manhattan. I don't like taking the chance of getting an uncomfortable cab for the long ride from Newark—and car services are not much more expensive.

My driver was waiting with a sea of other drivers holding signs just outside the security check. We walked through the baggage claim area—currently under renovation and a dim, crowded, tense scene. I felt victorious as I passed by the long taxi queue with my two small bags.

Once in the car, I paid with my credit card: $60, including tip and toll. Most car services range in price from $40 to $80. I've found cabs from Newark run in the $45 to $50 range. My driver was a kind, older Irish chap, with plenty of stories and a firm grip on the English language—rare in the case of most drivers these days.

The Surrey Hotel is on East 76th Street and Madison Avenue, just off Central Park. It's the nicest of the Manhattan East Suite Hotels group—mostly older no-name properties that have been spruced up to serve cost-conscious business travelers. My room was large and clean and had a fantastic view of the skyline; it included a small kitchenette, a two-line telephone, and a big bathroom. I liked the homey feel of the place—uncommon compared to previous hotel stays at big convention caverns or snooty pleasure palaces.

I only had a minute to throw my bags down, splash some water on my face, and run back out. I was meeting Wendy Perrin, an editor at *Condé Nast Traveler* magazine, at the *Triad Theatre* (212-362-2590) across the park on West 72nd to see the play *Secrets Every Smart Traveler Should Know*, based on a book she wrote.

After the play, Perrin and I jumped in a cab and shot across town to one of New York's latest, hippest restaurants, Asia de Cuba (212-726-7755). If you like the "see and be seen" scene, and can finagle a reservation, it's well worth the trip. The food is a delicious, exotic, and expensive fusion of Asian and Caribbean cuisine. Probably not the best place for a business meal, but a fantastic place to check the pulse of young, chic New York.

After a night like that, it was tough to face the day of meetings that followed. But the brisk walk to Rockefeller Center through a crackling cold and clear day, the smell of fire-roasted chestnuts and bus fumes, a peek at the tree in Rockefeller Center, all combined to make even a long day of meetings seem festive and fun. This is what *every* business trip should be like.

CHAPTER 4

Surviving the Airport

While airports have not historically ranked as anyone's favorite place, they *are* getting better. Remember the airports of yesteryear? Think beige, stuffy, low ceilings, frayed (or no) carpeting, linoleum, plastic bucket seats, ashtrays, sullen store clerks, Muzak, and overpriced, steam-table food. Airports used to look and feel a lot like office copiers: grayish and brutally functional. But all that is changing with the introduction of in-airport gyms, name-brand or fine dining, specialty shops, full-service bank branches, 24-hour ATMs, and even clinics and chapels. If the shopping mall has become the new town center of Middle America, the airport is now the town center for business travelers.

Airlines are tinkering with their airport operations and taking steps to make their flight schedules more reliable. They are speeding up the check-in process, requiring earlier check-in times, reducing advance boarding privileges, and cracking down on the number of carry-on bags allowed on the plane. While all of these changes are serving to minimize flight delays, it means that more responsibility is placed in the hands of the travelers. As always, there are certain predicaments that airlines can't avoid. Bad weather and air traffic congestion will continue to delay flights, no matter how efficient the airline itself is, but cooperation between airline and passenger definitely helps to speed up the process.

39—KNOW YOUR TRAVELER'S RIGHTS

Most business travelers know something about their rights at the airport. But much of what you may know is through hearsay or the occasional war story heard from a fellow traveler stuck in a scary situation. The following tips should provide you with the facts about your rights as travelers, and how to assert those rights when the need arises. You'll also find other general and safety tips that should help you survive any airport.

Since deregulation, government protection for air travelers is limited to three areas: limits of liability for lost and damaged luggage, rules for overbooking and bumping, and enforcement of the smoking ban on domestic flights. That's it. Outside of these three areas there is no other government protection. That means it's up to *you* to get what you deserve.

By law, the airlines must provide travelers with a copy of their contract of carriage upon request. If you are interested, contact the airlines' legal division and they will mail you one. Although a rare find, the contract should also (by law) be on hand at city ticket offices. You may not know it, but every time you buy an airline ticket, you are agreeing to the terms of these lengthy documents. A clever Web site, called "Rules of the Air" (www.rulesoftheair.com), maintains each airline's contract of carriage and explains the legalese in lay terms. If you ever run into a problem, this is a useful first place to look for help.

The best way to look out for your rights? First, know what they are (by reading this chapter, of course, or reading a contract of carriage). Second, if you feel your rights are being violated, *ask*. This is a major point: *always ask!* With deregulation the airlines are no longer required to offer any compensation for inconvenience. They are customer-oriented businesses, however, and they will try to help—but usually only upon request.

40—FLIGHT DELAYS

It's important to know that in their contracts of carriage, the airlines make *no guarantees* that they will get you to your destination on time, no matter what the reason. The *only* time you can expect any remuneration from an airline for not getting you to your destination on time is when you are *involuntarily* bumped.

Your first step in a delay should be to head to the nearest pay phone and find out *why* the flight is delayed. Ask the gate agents. Call the other airlines (don't waste your money, use their 800 numbers); see if *their* flights are experiencing similar delays. Look around at other gates. Are other flights leaving on time?

41—RULE 240 If you suspect that you are being delayed for something other than a weather or air traffic problem, approach the gate agent and confidently assert your suspicion, give a reason why you cannot wait, and ask to be booked on the next flight out on that airline *or a competing airline.* This is called Rule 240 and all the major airlines include it in their contract of carriage. (The terminology is from old CAB, or Civil Aeronautics Board jargon, when airlines were regulated.) If there are no acceptable flights available, the airline must refund your money, even if you are holding a "nonrefundable" ticket.

Rule 240 requires the original carrier to pick up the tab for any additional expense in getting you to your intended destination via another carrier. Rule 240 applies to other direct flights to your final destination as well as to any connecting flights that may exist. When you really want or need to get out of town, ask the gate agent: "Can you 240 me?" (It is important to use their lingo.) They should code your ticket, and you will be on your way.

Newfangled electronic tickets can present problems for those hoping to 240 their way out of a flight cancellation mess. In order to get coded over to another airline, you must first obtain a paper ticket from the original carrier (at the gate or customer service counter) before making arrangements with another carrier to accept your ticket.

42—GET THE GUIDE Refer to your *Official Airline Guide* (OAG) or other comprehensive schedule of all airlines to and from all destinations. These come in handy when you are trying to make a quick getaway from the mass confusion and hysteria that surrounds delay or cancellation announcements. (OAG, $96/year; tel: 800-323-3537. There is also an electronic edition of the OAG that you can load on your laptop.)

43—FLIGHT CANCELLATIONS

As in delay situations, go to an airport pay phone as soon as you hear a call for cancellation, and make a reservation on the next flight to your destination on that airline or a competing airline. Most of the time airline personnel will try to book everyone on *their* next flight out. Shrewd travelers know that the gate agents will put you on a *competitor's* next flight—but only if you ask. Sometimes you can build your own substitute itinerary via another airline or another hub better than the gate agent can. Go ahead and make suggestions.

Of course, the simplest way to avoid delay and cancellation situations is to fly airlines that maintain good on-time performance rankings. Or you can fly at times that the skies are not so congested. (Your chances of being delayed are greatest from 4 P.M. until 9 P.M.) Airline on-time performance rankings are made public each month by the Department of Transportation in its *Air Travel Consumer Report* (also on the Web at www.dot.gov). Flights are listed individually and by airline composite.

44—KNOW WHAT TO DO WHEN THE WEATHER DOES NOT COOPERATE

In most places, there will be times when Mother Nature just doesn't want to cooperate with your travel plans. So when a winter storm—or summer hurricane—is looming or in full force, keep these tips in mind.

- If it is already looking fierce outside, call before you leave for the airport and find out what the status is for your flight. Call your travel agent or the airline's automated arrival and departure line, or visit the airline's Web site, if available. Don't call the airline's toll-free reservations number for updates—you could be put on hold for too long.
- Keep your eye on the local news or the Weather Channel, or go to the Web site at www.weather.com or cnn.com/weather to find out if a storm is brewing in your area or destination. If bad weather looks likely, you may not want to leave for the airport until you've checked on your flight.
- If you are already at the airport and departure looks unlikely, try to make a reservation at a nearby hotel that offers free shuttle service. Don't wait too long, because airport hotels get booked up as fast as the flights are canceled.
- If it is absolutely essential that you make an out-of-town meeting or presentation when bad weather looms, consider leaving the night before. It is also wise to

take a cab or public transportation to the airport if a winter storm is a possibility, so you don't have to worry about digging your car out of the snow.

- Bring a snack along in the event that the airport food leaves something to be desired—or worse, in case the airport runs out of food (which has happened during unexpected storms). A bagel, pretzels, or dried fruits and nuts are nutritious, don't spoil, and don't take up a lot of space.
- Weather emergencies usually allow for airlines to relax rules when rerouting, changing, or cancellation fees are concerned.

45—GETTING BUMPED

To get your requested seat and avoid being bumped, you must obey the ticketing and check-in requirements spelled out in the contract of carriage of each airline in order to exercise your rights. While these vary from airline to airline, for most this means you must check in at the gate with positive ID at least 10-20 minutes before departure. You should get there at least 20 minutes before departure if you are not holding a boarding pass if you have only a phoned-in reservation or an electronic ticket. The 20-minute requirement is strict, and you must obey it if you want to assert your rights if you are bumped. (You are basically breaking your agreement with the airline if you can't get there on time. In that case, they can give your seat to someone else, and you'll get no compensation.)

46—SHOULD YOU VOLUNTEER?

The DOT requires airlines to ask for volunteers before denying booked passengers waiting for seats—what's known as *voluntary bumping*. Volunteers are entitled to whatever the airline offers them—usually a free round trip. However, many airlines offer only space-available or standby free tickets as their first offer to volunteers. These are difficult to use and cost the airline nothing to offer, so before you volunteer, make sure you are getting a confirmed, or "positive-space" round-trip ticket. Also, find out when or if the airline is going to book you on the *next* available flight out.

When ticket agents have to sweeten the pot to get volunteers, they are empowered to give cash, travel vouchers, and meal vouchers. Sometimes you can get free long-distance phone calls or a pass to the airline's airport club to wait for your next flight.

Another good time to consult your OAG (or the big airport flight monitors that list *all* flights) is when gate agents begin to ask for volunteers. If you find several other flights to your destination departing immediately after yours, volunteer, get your free ticket or other compensation, then ask to get booked on the next flight out.

47—GETTING BUMPED INVOLUNTARILY

If you are *involuntarily bumped* (meaning you have a reserved seat, have met the 20-minute cutoff, and the airline still denies you a seat), governmentally imposed protection kicks in. You can ask to be rebooked, or "240ed" on another airline. But if that flight gets you to your destination between one and two hours late, you are entitled to an amount equal to the price of your one-way fare, up to a maximum of $200. If you are more than two hours late, you are entitled to twice the value of your one-way ticket, up to a maximum of $400. Many times you can also keep your original ticket for a refund or future use. *Remember:* Bumping is more common during the holidays or busy summer months.

If there are several passengers who might be bumped waiting at the gate hoping to board, most airlines give top priority to first-class and business-class passengers, then to full-coach passengers and elite members of their frequent flier programs, then to everyone else.

Usually, the airlines will first try to appease those involuntarily bumped with free tickets. Depending on your situation, a free ticket might be more valuable than cash. But you won't get the cash unless you demand it. Perhaps better for frequent traveler program members is a travel voucher or a certificate of specific monetary value to apply to future flights on that airline. The voucher should always be worth at least the face value of the ticket you are holding. Travel vouchers are better for frequent travelers because you can still earn frequent flyer mileage on tickets "bought" in exchange for them. Travel on "free" bump coupons does not accrue frequent flier miles. (Unfortunately, not all airlines offer such vouchers; be sure to ask.)

48—LOST BAGS

Most business travelers prefer to carry their bags on the plane. But with airline cabins increasingly crowded, you may find yourself checking bags. And as we all know, checked bags get lost, damaged, or misplaced. Below are some facts that may help to minimize the nightmare of lost or delayed bags.

- One little-known fact is that airlines will reimburse you for out-of-pocket expenses associated with baggage delays. This usually includes toilet articles and some articles of clothing or some petty cash to buy them. You must ask for these things. (However, the amount of money that you spend will be deducted from the airline's final payment if your bag has been destroyed or is never recovered.)
- Fully 98 percent of all "misplaced" bags are returned to owners within hours. DOT regulations state that if the airline loses your bag, it is only required to reimburse you a maximum of $1250 for the depreciated value of the declared contents. (There is some discussion of raising this limit to $1850, but there has been no action as of early 1998.) Standard operating procedure is for the airlines to automatically depreciate your claim by 30 percent. International travelers are reimbursed for lost baggage based on the weight of their bags (under the Warsaw Convention). Currently, a paltry $9.07 *per pound* is all you'll get if your bags are lost on an international flight. So if your bags are lost and you are asked to estimate the value of the contents of your bags, err on the high side.

- To minimize really big losses buy excess valuation insurance when you check your bag. This typically costs about $1 per $100 in value that you declare—in excess of the $1250 automatic coverage. However, airlines claim no responsibility for many valuable items, including electronics, jewelry, or cameras, so *always* carry those items on board with you.
- If your bag is lost and you are traveling on a code-share flight, where you buy your ticket from one airline but get on the plane of another, the airline whose name is printed on your ticket is responsible for your compensation. However, the carrier that lost the bag should make a gallant effort to recover it first.

49—CHECK LUGGAGE TAGS AFTER AIRPORT GATE AGENT TIES THEM ON

Gate agents make mistakes, so be vigilant in double-checking that the your bags have the correct tag affixed to them. Those three-letter airport codes can be confusing. Some three-letter codes make perfect sense—Atlanta, for example is ATL—but many don't. The code for Knoxville, Tennessee, TYS, makes sense only if you know that the airport is named McGhee Tyson. Orlando's MCO comes from its original name, McCoy Field. Two unfortunate abbreviations: Sioux City, Iowa (SUX) and Fresno, California (FAT).

Here are some more airports with confusing codes.

BNA	Nashville
CVG	Cincinnati
DCA	Washington: Ronald Reagan National
IAD	Washington: Dulles
EWR	New York: Newark
LGA	New York: La Guardia
IAH	Houston: Intercontinental
ICT	Wichita, Kansas
MCI	Kansas City
MCO	Orlando
MSY	New Orleans
ORD	Chicago: O'Hare
SDF	Louisville, Kentucky
SNA	Orange County, California
YYZ	Toronto

50—KNOW HOW TO COMPLAIN . . .

Know *how* to complain (or compliment). When writing letters, remember that airline consumer affairs reps are deluged with piles of complaints—both real and off the wall. To maximize your chances of getting an answer or compensation, follow these tips.

- Keep your letter to one or two pages, typed, if possible.
- Spell out as concisely as possible exactly what happened, including dates, names, locations, and ticket or frequent flier numbers.
- Try not to be emotional—you'll lose credence. Wait a day or two after the incident to write the letter. The person reading the letter is trained in business, not counseling.

- If you want compensation, make your request as specific as possible. ("I'd like 5000 miles credited to my frequent flier account," for example.)

51—AND WHERE Send written complaints to U.S. Department of Transportation, C75, Room 4107, Washington, DC, 20590. To leave a comment recorded on voice mail with the DOT's Aviation Consumer Protection Division, call 202-366-2220. Complaints are charged against the airline in the DOT's monthly *Air Travel Consumer Report* (widely reported in the media) and serve as a basis for rule making and enforcement action.

Here are the telephone numbers and Web sites of the major airlines' consumer affairs offices.

Alaska: Seattle, WA	206-431-7286	www.alaska-air.com
America West: Phoenix, AZ	602-693-6019	www.americawest.com
American: Dallas, TX	817-967-2000	www.aa.com
Continental: Houston, TX	713-987-6500	www.flycontinental.com
Delta: Atlanta, GA	404-715-1450	www.delta-air.com
Northwest: St. Paul, MN	612-726-2046	www.nwa.com
Southwest: Dallas, TX	214-904-4223	www.iflyswa.com
TWA: St. Louis, MO	314-589-3600	www.twa.com
United: Chicago, IL	847-700-6796	www.ual.com
US Airways: Winston-Salem, NC	910-661-0061	www.usairways.com

52—HOW TO GET AN UPGRADE

Have you ever been upgraded to first-class for no special reason? Received a drink or a movie headset "on the house" from a friendly flight attendant? Most road warriors would agree that these little favors can make or break a business trip. When airports and airplanes are filled to the gills is when getting a break from an airline employee can really make a business trip a pleasure instead of an odyssey. But getting an upgrade is not as easy as it used to be. With the recent changes in frequent flier programs, first-class sections are usually full long before the day of the flight, making it harder for gate agents to do favors. There are too many legitimate ways for people to get up front.

So you want an upgrade? Here's some advice. The airport waiting list for upgrades or standby seats is *not* compiled on a first-come, first-served basis. It is based on a formula of frequent flier program status, the fare you paid, and whether or not you are in an emergency situation. However, you should not arrive at the gate five minutes before the plane is scheduled to depart and expect to be upgraded. By this time, officials are too rushed to do anyone a favor.

53—JUST BE NICE

- Don't get loud and make demands. Treat the gate agent like a human being and turn on the charm. Most gate agents claim that the nice travelers—those who treat them with dignity and respect—are most likely to get results. If a first-class seat pops up at the last minute, the agent will most likely remember the passenger who was nice.

- "Charm" your way into first class. This tactic works best when the flight is not full and there's not a covey of high-status frequent fliers huddling around the gate pressing for upgrades. Dress nicely. Be cool, charming, and inquisitive. Try subtle bribery—compliment the agent on the professional way he or she is handling the crowd that day. Some travelers go to extremes, like giving gate agents roses from airport concourse vendors, or presenting a box of donuts to a morning gate crew. Don't laugh—it works!
- Make the agent aware of any special circumstances. Agents can look at your record (the PNR) in the computer and see that, for example, you've been on five of that airline's flights over the last three days, two of which were delayed. Or maybe you've just returned from a round-the-world trip. Agents will sometimes see what they can do for a passenger in this type of situation.
- Don't make a big deal about how many frequent flier miles you have. Most gate computer screens display your mileage status next to your frequent flier number, so they automatically know if you are an "elite" member—usually in the top 3 to 5 percent of fliers. Better to let the agent discover your status instead of announcing it or bragging about it.

Usually, the biggest talkers have the fewest miles.

54—GENERAL AIRPORT TIPS

- Join an airline club, a true refuge from the mob scenes that sometimes form at airports. These are excellent places to avoid having to wait in line for your ID to be checked, for seat assignment changes, or for other ticketing problems. Many provide complimentary cocktails, beverages, and snacks. (Delta's Crown Room and Northwest's World Club are the only ones to offer free cocktails universally.) Beware, though: hub-and-spoke systems have caused many clubs to be overcrowded, especially during airport rush hours. In 1998, the first year of membership in United's Red Carpet Club is $400 or 50,000 miles for nonpremier frequent flier members and $275 or 40,000 miles for premier members. American Airline's clubs cost $300 or 50,000 frequent flier miles; Delta is $300 or 30,000 miles and Northwest is $270. Continental comes in at $200, while TWA is $175 or 30,000 miles. Most also offer spouse and domestic partner memberships at various prices.
- If you don't want to drop all those bucks or miles for an airport club membership, consider a day pass. Many airlines will allow you to buy trial or daylong memberships for anywhere from $30 to $60. Just walk in and ask.

- Your airline ticket is composed of coupons good for each segment of your journey. Check your ticket as your board to ensure that only the correct coupon has been removed by the gate agent.
- Make sure there's space at the airport parking lot. There's nothing worse than rushing to the airport at the last minute only to find the "sold out" sign going up. Call ahead to determine lot availability if you can, take a taxi or public transportation, or arrange to be dropped off. Also, be prepared for long lines to pay at airport parking check-out booths, which are usually worse Sunday evening or after a long weekend.

55—LAPTOP TIPS

Surveys show that about 60 percent of business travelers tote their laptops around with them when they travel. Here are some tips from *Batteries* catalog (800-228-8374) to help make computing on the road or on the fly a little bit easier.

- X-ray machines do not create a magnetic pulse, so they are not harmful to laptops, cassette tapes, or other electronically stored data. In Eastern Europe, the former Soviet Union, and many other less developed countries, however, the motors that drive the conveyer belts through the X-ray machine may not be adequately shielded, which does pose a danger. To minimize risk, place your laptop in the center of the belt, or ask that your equipment be manually inspected.

- The metal detectors you must walk through create a strong magnetic pulse that may erase the contents of your hard drive. Never let your laptop near the metal detector, and don't forget to remove any floppy disks from your pocket before going through.
- Watch out for reclining seats. The indentation on the seat in front of you for stowing the tray table can be your laptop's and your wallet's worst enemy if your laptop screen gets caught by a sudden recliner. To avoid this expensive repair, pull your laptop as close to you as possible. Alternatively, use the in-flight magazine as a buffer by standing it vertically behind your laptop screen.
- In flight, aircraft are pressurized at approximately 8500 feet. This can cause printer cartridges to leak. Save yourself the mess and damage by wrapping the cartridges in plastic.

56—LEAVE YOUR LAPTOP AT HOME

There are plenty of people who really need all the power of a laptop PC in their briefcase. But if you use your laptop as nothing more than a communications device—a way to read and send e-mail or connect to the Internet when you're away from the office—you might not need to lug along all that extra weight. There are a growing number of places to stop along the way and connect to the Web; these are known as *public Internet access facilities*, or PIAFs.

These so-called cyberbooths—workstations, booths, kiosks, and desktop Internet devices located in public areas like airports and hotel lobbies—offer Internet access to anyone. There are also trendy "cybercafes" in many major cities, offering coffee, food, and computers for public use.

At airports the cost ranges from 25 to 33 cents per minute (in 1998), with the swipe of most major credit cards. Hotels offering PCs with in-room Internet access charge $10 to $25 per day. Others, like the cybercafes, Kinko's, or Mail Boxes Etc, charge about $7 to $15 per hour.

57—PLAY IT SAFE! BEWARE OF DANGERS IN THE PARKING LOT

Major-city airports do not usually volunteer the increasing number of airport parking lot crimes to the public. Try to park in well-lighted spaces only a short walk from the terminal building—even if it costs more. A safer option would be to use the new privately operated off-airport lots that have sprung up recently. These lots are usually well tended and offer regular shuttle service between your car and the main terminal.

58—WATCH OUT FOR THIEVES IN PRIME AREAS

- Stay on your guard at the airport curbside skycap stand, restroom stalls, phone banks, security checkpoints, and the baggage claim area.
- Don't let your bags out of your sight for a minute. It only takes a second for a crook to walk off with your possessions.

At the baggage claim, stand with your bags in front of you. There is no uniform rule that security agents at exit doors must match baggage claim tickets with stubs. Some airports offer this service, some don't.

- Never hang purses, coats, or other belongings on the door hooks of restroom stalls. All a thief needs to do is reach over the door and grab them while you are preoccupied. Instead, place them around your neck, or on the floor between your feet.
- Thieves often operate in teams at security checkpoints. One will distract you and security personnel by setting off the metal detector while the other grabs your bags as they exit the x-ray conveyor belt. Wait until the person in front of you has cleared security before you place your luggage on the conveyer belt.
- Always keep an eye on your laptop, cell phone, or pager. Electronic gear, which experienced thieves can spot in a second, is easy to sell on the black market.

59—LABEL BAGS INSIDE AND OUTSIDE

Outside tags have a tendency to be shorn from bags in airport luggage-handling systems. Best to label your bag inside and out. Some business travelers prefer to list their business address only. Listing a home address could lead to a burglary if the scoundrel that took your bag also wants to hit your house.

60—BEWARE OF TELEPHONE CALLING CARD THIEVES

Watch out for "shoulder surfers," or people who steal your long-distance calling card number by spying on you at airports. Be especially wary when using the "calling card only" phones, which are targeted by these creeps. My calling card number was stolen, or "surfed," at San Francisco Airport when I placed some long-distance calls from a pay phone in early 1997. The thief watched me enter my calling card number, recorded it, then sold it to a ring. Within two hours, my calling card number had been transmitted to prisoners in a corrections institution, among others, who made almost $500 in calls to Australia, Morocco, and a handful of other places before the MCI computers automatically deactivated it, leaving me with no calling card for a couple days.

Shoulder surfers are more prevalent in cities with large immigrant populations, which provide a perfect market for stolen calling cards. Some phones now have special shields to thwart prying eyes, but if not, cover the phone with your body when entering your number, or if possible, swipe your card through the reader on the phone. Speak quietly if you must dictate your number to an operator.

61—EXPECT DELAYS AT SECURITY CHECKPOINTS DURING CRISES

Remember the long lines and extra hassles during the Gulf War in early 1991? Just wait for the next international crisis—it will happen again. Plan on arriving at the airport ahead of time. Expect to see more thermal neutron scanners or sniffers; they will eliminate the need to search bags and help speed up this process. And in the meantime, be grateful for security vigilance. Don't hassle your inspector. Proper screening of all passengers could save many lives.

Here are some other tips to help you get through the process smoothly.

- New bag-matching requirements that went into effect in 1998 can slow things down. Be sure your electronic gear has working batteries: you'll probably be asked to turn your unit on.
- Don't pack guns, knives, or potential weapons in carry-on bags. Believe it or not, people forget that they have weapons in the bottom of their purse or briefcase. Also, toy guns and knives brought home to kids do not amuse security personnel. Mace or pepper spray canisters are also verboten. Best to pack these items in your checked luggage.
- Don't leave bags unattended. Unattended bags are prime bomb suspects. Unattended bags on British ferries are thrown overboard. At Israeli airports, they are incinerated.
- Move quickly away from bomb scenes. In the event of an airport bomb, move away from the scene as quickly as possible. Serious terrorists typically plant two bombs—the second as a backup if the first fails.

62—KEEP AN EYE ON THE FUTURE

As airports revamp to meet the demands of the future, they offer novel, and even luxurious, amenities to travelers. Here are some examples.

- **Chicago's O'Hare Airport** helps to make the best of a bad situation, like getting delayed or snowed in. For $9 a visit, the O'Hare Hilton Health Club offers a place to work out and relax while you're waiting for your flight.
- The **Air Canada Maple Leaf Lounge at Edmonton Airport** has a crackling fireplace and Banff Brewery beer on tap. It's almost enough to make you want to be snowed in.
- If you've got a craving for some mean Southern cooking, check out one of the two Paschal's restaurants located in **Atlanta's Hartsfield Airport**. At one time this Atlanta institution was frequented by Martin Luther King, Jr. It serves soulful favorites like grits and eggs, turnip greens, barbecued ribs, hot biscuits, and fried chicken.
- Take the elevator at **Miami International Airport** to the top floor of the Miami International Hotel and enjoy a spectacular view, snacks from the bar, a drink, or a workout in the sauna, gym, or pool, or on the rooftop running track.
- **Orlando International** is home to a 20-barrel microbrewery and two Shipyard BrewPub restaurants.

- Relax and enjoy a facial from an in-house beauty therapist, practice golf on the indoor green, get a haircut, ski on a 3-D downhill simulator, or kick back and listen to CDs in the music conservatory at the Virgin Atlantic Clubhouse inside **London's Heathrow Airport**.
- Eat oysters on the half shell or steamed lobster at the Legal Sea Foods restaurant in **Boston's Logan Airport** or the new terminal at **Washington's Ronald Reagan National Airport**. There's also a retail market where you can order a live lobster or some famous New England clam chowder.

An Urban Myth with a Lesson

The following item made the rounds of frequent fliers' e-mail boxes around the country in 1997. The original source is unknown.

An award should go to a United Airlines gate agent in Denver for being smart and funny, and for making her point, when confronted with a passenger who probably deserved to fly as cargo.

During the final days at Denver's old Stapleton Airport, a crowded United flight was canceled. A single agent was rebooking a long line of inconvenienced travelers. Suddenly an angry passenger pushed his way to the front of the line. He slapped his ticket down on the counter and said, "I *have* to be on this flight and it has to be *first class*." The agent replied, "I'm sorry sir. I'll be happy to try to help you, but I've got to help these folks first, and I'm sure we'll be able to work something out."

The passenger was unimpressed. He asked loudly, so that the passengers behind him could hear, "Do you have any idea who I am?"

Without hesitating, the gate agent smiled and grabbed her public address microphone.

"May I have your attention, please?" she began, her voice bellowing throughout the terminal. "We have a passenger here at the gate *who does not know who he is*. If anyone can help him find his identity, please come to gate 17."

With the folks behind him in line laughing hysterically, the man glared at the United agent, gritted his teeth, and swore, "#$%& you!"

Without flinching, she smiled and said, "I'm sorry, sir, but you'll have to stand in line for that, too."

The man retreated as the people in the terminal applauded loudly. Although the flight was canceled and people were late, they were no longer angry at United.

CHAPTER 5

On the Plane

In his story "Travels with a Donkey," Robert Louis Stevenson claims, "For my part, I travel not to go anywhere, but to go. I travel for travel's sake. The great affair is to move." Travel has come a long way since Stevenson's era, when beasts of burden were a primary mode of transportation. However, many of us still have a great affair with moving. These days the preferred mode is jet aircraft. Here are some tips to make those high-altitude moves a little easier.

63—GET THE BEST SEATS: ON DOMESTIC FLIGHTS . . .

Most major carriers now reserve "priority seating," or window and aisle seats, near the front of the plane for higher-mileage members of their frequent flier programs. But occasionally gate agents will seat parents traveling with infants in the bulkhead, or front-row seats, especially on longer international flights. Beware of this during the heavy summer or holiday periods.

Better bet: ask for an exit row seat where babies aren't allowed. The FAA requires a few extra inches between these seats (usually over the wing) to facilitate an emergency evacuation. The FAA also requires that those who sit in exit row seats speak English and are physically able and willing to remove the emergency door and assist other passengers in the event of an evacuation. The downside is that these seats do not always recline. The ability to reserve exit row seats ahead of time varies from airline to airline, with frequent flier status playing a role in determining who gets them.

All planes are not created equal. When an airline orders new planes or refurbishes older ones, the airline (not the manufacturer) determines how wide the seats will be and how much legroom they'll allow. Therefore, comfort levels on the same models vary from airline to airline.

If you are traveling with someone else and are reserving a seat on a plane with a three-abreast configuration, book the two outer (aisle and window) seats. If the plane is not full, the likelihood of the airline reserving the middle seat is slim.

Don't want to be chatted to death by your seatmate? Put on a set of Walkman headphones, even if you are not listening to them.

64—AND ON INTERNATIONAL FLIGHTS, TOO

If you haven't flown in business or first class on an international flight lately, you're in for a surprise. As the airlines' financial results brighten, they are finally making improvements for those of us who are helping the turnaround more than anyone else—business travelers flying at the front end of the plane.

Many airlines have followed the prescient lead of Virgin Atlantic Airways, which in 1984 decided to scrap first class and enhance business class, offering first-class service at a business-class price with their trendsetting Upper Class cabin. It took almost 10 years, but Continental was the next airline to embrace the concept of first-class service at a business-class price with its hybrid BusinessFirst section. Continental's upgraded cabin offers roomy, electronically controlled sleeper seats with almost 6 feet between each, upgraded food service, and personal in-flight entertainment systems. With the rising popularity of services like Continental's BusinessFirst among the transatlantic cognoscenti, other airlines are jumping on the bandwagon with similar concepts. So far, KLM, Northwest, TWA, SAS, Sabena, USAir, Alitalia, and Air Canada have switched to similar hybrid business class–economy class configurations.

Although the line is blurring between business and first class, there is still a market for the true high-end travelers. Recognizing this, British Airways, Air France, Lufthansa, and others have taken the bold step of completely reconfiguring their first-class cabins and providing passengers with the ultimate in comfort: beds. Air France's L'Espace 180 features new seats that, when fully reclined, are 180 degrees flat and 6½ feet long. Between each seat is an optional privacy divider that rolls up when it's time to nod off. British Airways' more radical departure from the standard 2 x 2 seat configuration is actually an individual, semiprivate "pod" with a seat for the passenger, a small table, and a smaller seat for a visitor. Upgraded food and wine on both carriers are completely à la carte and on demand. (The least they could do for a $5,000 to $10,000 round-trip ticket, no?) To leap ahead of stiff transatlantic competition, Virgin Atlantic plans to install *bunk beds* in the belly of its new Airbus A340s, along with showers and an exercise and massage area, by 2002.

65—DINING WELL ON AIRLINE FOOD

Airline food is a frequent and easy target of business traveler wrath and ridicule. Come on, folks, a stainless steel galley hurtling through the stratosphere at 500 miles per hour is not the most convenient place to prepare a dinner banquet for 200. Frankly, it's amazing what some in-flight kitchens can turn out.

Recently, airlines have returned to the basics with their in-flight coach-class fare focusing on perfectly satisfying meals like salads, turkey on a croissant, fresh carrots, an apple, or a bagel. While some business travelers sniff at the trend toward brown-bag pickup at the gate, what's inside the bag is better than before. Hot meals are reserved for only the longest flights. And business-class and first-class meals are constantly updated and changed, with a new celebrity chef or regional cuisine introduced every season.

The hottest trend in international business class is a simple concept: the snack bar. Continental offers "cookie jar service," where passengers can snack on Toblerone chocolates, fruit, cheeses, and cookies throughout the flight. British Airways and American Airlines have similar services, called "Raid the Larder" and "Snack Attack," respectively.

66—GETTING WHAT YOU LIKE TO EAT Most airlines offer a wide array of unpublicized special meals that are usually an improvement over the standard fare. Delta's seafood platter is a favorite among frequent travelers. American Airlines offers healthy-heart meals, approved by the American Heart Association. United Airlines offers McDonald's Happy Meals, consisting of cheeseburgers, sausage and biscuits, cookies, and a toy for both adults and children. Midwest Express Airlines actually bakes chocolate chip cookies in-flight and serves them in the aroma-filled cabin.

Requests for special in-flight meals have become de rigueur among many business travelers with restricted diets, or just a taste for something different. All airlines offer a kosher meal, which is usually fresher and more wholesome than the standard fare. Interestingly, the Muslim meal is almost identical to the kosher meal—only without a rabbi's blessing. The Hindu meal consists of vegetables that grow above the ground and is usually seasoned with curry. Vegetarian meals feature whole-grain bread, fresh fruit, and vegetables. Here's a standard list of meal options.

- Bland
- Child
- Diabetic
- Fruit
- Hindu
- Kosher
- Lacto-ovo vegetarian

- Low-calorie
- Low/no fat and cholesterol
- Low/no sodium
- Nonvegetarian Muslim
- Seafood
- Strict vegetarian
- Vegetarian Muslim

67—GETTING WHAT YOU ORDERED

- Request a special meal through your travel agent or reservationist at least 24 hours before your flight. Since these requests are often overlooked, be sure to follow up on your request by calling ahead on the day of your flight, and again when you check in.
- Be kind. Flight attendants never seem to be very happy about serving special meals. It takes more time and effort to prepare these meals and get the right meal to the right person.
- Check your flight's meal options when you make your reservation. Your meal options and food quality expand if you can get on the first, or domestic, leg of an international flight—that is, a flight from Atlanta to Los Angeles that continues on to Tokyo. Also, many transcontinental flights have upgraded food offerings.

68—CARE FOR YOUR EARS IN-FLIGHT

The rapid changes in altitude and air pressure associated with takeoff and landing can wreak havoc with your inner ear. You can avoid serious problems by following a few simple steps on every flight.

- If you are suffering from a cold or another malady that causes nasal congestion, take a decongestant or nasal spray before your flight. For long flights, take it again about an hour before landing.
- Keep a mentholated inhaler in your briefcase during cold and flu season.
- If you feel excess pressure in your ears, open your eustachian tubes by yawning or swallowing. If this fails to alleviate the pressure, pinch your nostrils closed and use your cheek and throat muscles to force a mouthful of air against your lips and nostrils. Using your chest and stomach muscles with this maneuver could create too much pressure.
- Chew gum or ice.
- A loud pop in your ears should signal an end to your discomfort. However, if the problem persists, see your physician.
- Consider a product called Earplanes, two small plastic plugs that equalize the pressure inside and outside your ears. These are available at many travel and luggage stores or in catalogs like Magellan's (800-962-4943).

69—USE IN-FLIGHT GADGETS TO WORK AND PLAY

Most airlines are now outfitting their aircraft with new passenger communications and entertainment systems. These digital (versus analog) in-flight systems allow passengers to send and receive static-free voice and data calls; get airport gate information; make car, hotel, and airline reservations; find out news and weather headlines; retrieve stock quotes; play video games; and even access the Internet.

The World Airline Entertainment Association says that airlines spent $1.4 billion on in-flight entertainment in 1997—that's up from $400 million in 1992. The cutting edge in this field is video on demand. Passengers can start and stop movies as they please—no more pilot interruptions at the movie's key moment. Viewing is on *your* schedule. You'll find on-demand systems on newer aircraft only.

Many of these new systems now offer in-flight gambling, with wins and losses paid to or from the passenger's credit card. To protect against major losses, most airlines limit winnings to about $2000 and losses to about $200.

Some major carriers are installing in-seat power plugs for business and first-class passengers. But you can't plug into the seatback like you'd plug into the wall in your home or office. In most cases, you have to purchase a special plug that costs about $100. And as with any new technology, there are kinks, which include reservationists not knowing which aircraft have the outlets, problems getting the correct cords to connect, and equipment malfunctions. But in the near future, when these problems are addressed, you may never have to lug along a (*HEAVY!*) extra battery again!

70—KNOW ABOUT IN-FLIGHT NO-NO'S

In the early nineties, the airlines banned the use of laptop computers or CD players during takeoff and landing. Although there is no clear evidence that a GameBoy could bring down a 747, no one wants to take any chances. You can still use your laptop once the pilot turns off the seat belt sign and announces that the aircraft has reached cruising altitude. However, you must turn your unit off when the seat belt sign goes back on, signaling descent and landing.

The use of cellular phones is also prohibited while the plane is airborne. Cell phone calls placed from the air can wreak havoc on ground-based cellular networks and may be harmful to the electromagnetic properties of the plane itself.

71— UNDERSTAND FEAR OF FLYING

If you are aerophobic (a fearful flier), select a seat at the front of the plane, where the ride is smoother and quieter. Talk to the person in the next seat. Recognize that your anxieties are okay, but don't focus on them.

What do aerophobics dread most? Crashing and burning is at the top of the list. Interestingly, losing control and having to be physically subdued once the plane takes off is the second biggest fear. Other fears include claustrophobia and worrying that the pilot may have a heart attack and lose control of the aircraft.

Put your fears in perspective.

- Each year in the United States, 40,000 people die in car accidents. In 1985, one of the worst years for aviation fatalities, 525 people died. More people die in car accidents in just three months than have died in plane crashes since the dawn of aviation.

- There are a lot of activities that are more dangerous than flying. For example, the National Safety Council says that each year, about 12,000 Americans die from accidental falls; 5,600 from poisoning; 4,600 from drowning; and 1,400 from accidental shootings.
- While the number of flights performed around the world has more than doubled in the last 15 years, the fatal accident rate for passenger aircraft is not significantly higher.

If your fears are still not allayed, here's what you can do.

- Choose first-world airlines with good safety records, younger fleets, and larger planes.
- Avoid small propeller-driven aircraft when possible. Statistics prove that in a crash, the larger the plane, the more likely there are to be survivors.
- Listen to the on-board safety announcement and make a mental note of the emergency exit nearest your seat. Many airline accidents occur while the plane is on the ground, and a quick evacuation can save your life.
- Fly nonstop, if possible. Since most accidents happen during takeoff, landing, and taxi, a nonstop flight is the safest.

72—GET SOME HELP

Fear of flying is a deep-seated problem that this book alone cannot solve. If the problem persists and threatens your livelihood, call your local Mental Health Association for a list of psychologists that specialize in the treatment of phobias, or try one of the following programs.

- The Pegasus Fear of Flying Foundation, made up of a group of active pilots and practicing psychologists, provides a one-day total immersion program, multimedia self-help tape kits ($75), and even one-on-one therapy. Pegasus claims a 100 percent success rate. Call 800-FEAR-NOT (800-332-7668), or see their Web site at www.pegasus-fear-fly.com.
- American Airlines regularly schedules a series of two-day Fearless Flyer classes in various cities around the country. The fee includes a round-trip graduation flight. For information, call 817-424-5108.
- See the San Francisco-based Fear of Flying Clinic Web site at www.fofc.com.

73—BRUSH UP ON IN-FLIGHT ETIQUETTE

"Do unto others . . ." is probably the best piece of advice to keep in mind where in-flight etiquette is concerned. Here are some more mannerly tips.

- Obey rear-to-front boarding instructions, especially if you have any unwieldy carry-on bags.
- Try to use only the space above your seat for your carry-ons. If that is not possible, then at least try to stow your bag above

the rows ahead of you. This prevents you from going against traffic when you have to retrieve your bag once the plane has landed.

- Do your best to avoid blocking the aisle when stowing your bag in the overhead bin. If you are having a problem, let other passengers get by.
- When stowing a large bag in the overhead bin, remove any soft items, coats, or hats already placed there. Then neatly fold and replace items on top or alongside your bag.
- If you have any items that may break or leak, place them under the seat in front of you. The same goes for any particularly heavy items, like laptop computers.
- Remember, underseat storage means under the seat in front of you, not under your own seat. Bulkhead seats (facing the wall) do not have any underseat storage space. All carry-ons must go in the overhead for takeoff and landing.
- Help short, weak, or infirm passengers stow their bags.
- If you need assistance, politely ask the flight attendant and be patient, especially during boarding.

74—CAREFUL WITH THAT BAG!

The newfangled wheeled carry-on luggage, increasingly popular with business travelers, presents a new problem: those dirty wheels. Passengers drag these bags across the floors of airports, city streets, and bathrooms.

Then they drag them on the plane and throw them in the overhead bins—up against pillows, sweaters, and coats. Also, most wheeled carry-ons are larger and harder than conventional bags; many barely fit overhead *or* under the seat. Another problem, especially with the older DC-9s and 727s built *before* the days of the carry-on craze: the overhead bins are about as big as toaster ovens. Bins on newer aircraft like the MD-11 are the size of giant ice chests.

75—MAKE YOUR FLIGHT AS COMFORTABLE AS POSSIBLE

Business trips can be stressful. You run to make your flight at the last minute. You are forced to sit in a cramped, uncomfortable seat for long periods of time. Air pressure changes affect your inner ear; and stale cabin air dries your skin, lips, and nose. Give your body a break on the plane by following these next few tips.

- Sitting with your legs crossed restricts blood circulation. If you've got room, use your carry-on luggage as a footrest to elevate your feet. Get up every hour or so and stretch out your tired, cramped leg muscles.
- Support your neck with a pillow while you sleep. Create an ergonomically correct seat by placing a pillow in the small of your back.
- Wear glasses instead of contact lenses during the flight.
- Fill a small atomizer with water to spray on your face. It serves as a moisturizer and a refresher.

76—WHAT DO BUSINESS TRAVELERS WANT?

According to a 1997 *Official Airline Guide* survey of 2250 business travelers from nine countries, the most important in-flight features are, in descending order of importance:

1. Legroom
2. Angle of seat recline
3. Food service on demand
4. Seatback or hand-held video
5. Pillows and blankets
6. In-flight beds
7. Telephones
8. On-board business facilities

And here's what business travelers say they do most on seemingly interminable flights (in descending order).

1. Sleep.
2. Read.
3. Work.
4. Watch movies.
5. Eat and drink.
6. Listen to music.
7. Talk with passengers.

77—PAY ATTENTION TO RANKINGS

Wondering which airline will give you the most bang for your buck? According to a 1997 Zagat Airline Survey, you'll have to go halfway across the globe to find it. For four years in a row, Singapore Airlines has earned the top ranking among international airlines, and other Asian and Pacific carriers dominate the top 10. Here's the list.

1. Singapore Airlines
2. Cathay Pacific
3. Swissair
4. Japan Airlines
5. Thai Airways
6. ANA-All Nippon Airways
7. Qantas
8. Air New Zealand
9. SAS
10. Virgin Atlantic

Zagat's top 10 domestic airlines are:

1. Midwest Express
2. Alaska
3. American
4. United
5. Delta
6. Kiwi
7. Midway
8. Reno Air
9. Northwest
10. Aloha

78—PLAY IT SAFE IN-FLIGHT

Even if you're not a member of the white-knuckle crowd, be aware of basic in-flight safety measures.

- *Sit in the rear of the plane for safety.* Although it is difficult to say where the safest place to sit on a plane is, aircraft manufacturers put the black box, or in-flight recorder, in the tail of the plane—the place they feel is least likely to be destroyed in an accident.

- *Sit over the wing for stability.* If you are prone to motion sickness, a seat over the wing ensures the smoothest ride.
- *Keep your seat belt fastened at all times.* Even when the pilot says that it's okay to move about the cabin, keep your seat belt fastened. Unexpected clear-air turbulence could cause you and anything else in the cabin to hit the ceiling without warning. Keep your seat belt fastened around your hips and below your stomach, so that your body will pivot if you are thrown forward and the belt will not cause internal injury.
- *Choose safety-conscious airlines with newer fleets.* A survey of airline passengers by the Switzerland-based International Foundation of Airline Passenger Associations (IFAPA) revealed that El Al, Swissair, Lufthansa, Qantas, and Delta are the international carriers perceived as "most safety conscious." During international crises these carriers usually report that their business and first-class bookings remain steady while other airlines experience declines.
- *Read the safety card, listen to the pre-flight announcement, and plan your exit.* Interviews with air-crash survivors show that reading those "international language" safety cards, mentally noting the nearest exits, and planning an escape route *before* takeoff were factors in their survival. Just do it!

- *If possible, fly jets and avoid propeller-driven aircraft.* The higher likelihood of crashes on propeller-driven aircraft has prompted many regional airlines to switch to jets, which should serve to enhance both the comfort and safety of your flight. If jet service is not available, however, avoid flying at night or in bad weather.
- *Don't try to sneak smokes in the bathroom.* Fires from bathroom trash bins have been on the rise ever since the smoking ban went into effect.

Confessions of a Frequent Traveler: Hong Kong

We've all heard what the experts say about maintaining a positive mental attitude. When you are faced with a 24-hour journey to the other side of the world, a well-honed positive attitude comes in handy.

While many people may feel that a transpacific flight is something to endure, I was determined to make it something I'd enjoy. Here's a chronicle of the highlights of a trip from Atlanta to Hong Kong. Come on along. . . .

Hour 1: On-board flight from Atlanta to New York. Can't stop thinking about the fact that it's 4:30 P.M. here and 5:30 A.M. in Hong Kong. A new day is beginning on the other side of the world, but it's just late afternoon here. The best part about this leg of my trip? The view of the sun setting to the west as this old Delta Boeing 727 soars over a sparkling clear New York City skyline.

Hour 3: At JFK Airport in New York. Mayhem reigns as passengers arrive for the bank of early evening departures. Cars are lined up two deep, horns honking, cab drivers shouting. Ah, New York! What's best about JFK? The people watching. An international crossroads like no other in the world. What a show!

Hour 4: I check in for my Cathay Pacific flight to Hong Kong. The business-class lounge, which Cathay shares with Delta, is full. Ignoring cautions to avoid alcohol before a long international flight, I order a vodka tonic and practice my Spanish with the Colombian bartender. Make one final call home, check my voice mail, then hook up my laptop and download my e-mail to read on the flight.

Hour 5: Trundle down the terminal to the gate with my wheeled bag and briefcase. Here's a nice opening touch: business-class and first-class passengers board through a separate jetway leading to the front of the aircraft. That means we can get right on board and bypass the huddled masses entering the coach section.

Hour 6: On-board. One thing that I've learned from my international travel experiences is to change my watch, as well as my mind, to the destination time zone as soon as I sit down. So, while it's 9 P.M. in New York and Atlanta, it's 10 A.M. in Hong Kong. Using a sort of mental imagery I've learned in my battles with jet lag, I take a moment to envision the sun rising on a misty morning, birds singing, coffee brewing.

Hour 7: It's a dark night on the cold plains beneath us as we fly to Vancouver. I'm seated in one of the best seats in business class, a bulkhead window. And I'm on everyone's favorite aircraft, a 747-400. And with my nice big business-class seat (home for the next 20 hours), I get an in-seat audio-video system with eight channels of video, extendable footrest, and new built-in-the-headrest "wings" to hold my head in position (and prevent drooling!) while sleeping.

Hour 9: Service from the small army of flight attendants is doting—hot towels, menus, they even address each of us by name. One of the nice things about 747s is that there is plenty of room to walk around and keep the circulation moving. However, it's hard to get out of business class for a full tour of the plane, as velcro-lined curtains separate us from the cloistered, cushy, caviared confines of the first-class cabin.

Hour 11: Vancouver Airport. Enjoyed watching the lighted ski slopes of the Whistler Resort as we landed. Cathay's swank business-class lounge offers the usual goodies *and* a touch of things to come: dim sum in a bamboo steamer and hot tea.

Hour 13: Back on board. The in-flight amenity kit put together by Caswell and Massey offers wax ear plugs, an all-cotton eye mask, and a Do Not Disturb sticker, among other items. I take off my shoes, push my seat into a full recline, extend the footrest, and pop my sleeping pill. You see, I'm one of those who have a very hard time sleeping on planes. Last year, I discovered a prescription drug called Ambien that has no hangover effect. Good night. (Or is it good morning? Whatever!)

Hour 19: Six or seven hours later. I awake to the smell of another meal service, peel off the eyemask, pull the wax out of my ears, look down at my watch. *Yes!! I Win!*

Almost seven hours of sleep! I will survive my first day on the other side of the world!

Hour 20: By simply asking permission of the purser, I am invited to sit in the cockpit jumpseat as we approach Japan. It's still black as ink outside, but there are a few lights on the horizon ahead. "It's the Japanese fishing fleet out on their morning runs," explains the Zimbabwean captain. I ask him what is the best view he's ever seen from the cockpit. "Flying over Afghanistan in the morning when it's a clear day," he says, smiling. "Nothing like it in the world."

Hour 24: On approach to Hong Kong's Kai Tak Airport, we fly over Lantau Island and the site of Chek Lap Kok Airport, undoubtedly the next best airport in the world.

Hour 25: On the ground. Now, if I can only make it to the hotel for a hot shower and a nap, I can recharge my batteries for my first day of meetings!

CHAPTER 6

On the Road

Business Travel. The term evokes images of dark-suited men and women confidently moving from limousine to airport lounge to airplane first-class cabin to glass office building to luxury hotel.

But with airfares higher than ever, especially on short commuter hops served by a single airline, business travel is becoming a much more down-to-earth affair. For many, it's more likely that a business trip will take place in a Buick instead of a Boeing.

You've made it through the friendly skies. Now it's time to hit the road. Whether you rent a car in conjunction with a flight or you drive your own car on business, this chapter is for you.

79—KNOW THE PLAYERS

- Avis, Budget, Hertz, and National are the largest car rental companies with the most on-airport locations. These full-service operators have frequent airport shuttle services to close-in lots, in-airport counters, express services that drop you off at your car, and technological amenities like dash-mounted global-positioning satellite systems. But they are also the most expensive. If you value convenience over price, choose one of the big four.

- Smaller players, like Alamo, Dollar, Payless, and Thrifty, offer standard rates that are about 25 percent less than the large players, but you get fewer frills. Here you can expect longer waits at trigger points like the airport shuttle or the counter where you pick up or drop off your car. Also, you can expect bigger crowds and longer waits during peak vacation seasons (spring break, late summer, and Christmas) when business travelers compete for cars with the price-sensitive leisure travel crowd.

80—SHOP AROUND FOR CAR RENTAL DEALS

One of the best deals in business travel has always been the rental car. It used to be cheaper to rent a car for a day than to rent a tuxedo, ski equipment, or even a bicycle. The reason: stiff competition and overcapacity. With too many cars chasing too few renters, rates remained flat. But all that is changing as the car rental industry consolidates. With the specter of increasing rates, it pays to be a smart buyer. Here are some pointers.

- Basic rates may not seem higher than before, but add-ons like additional driver fees, drop-off fees, peak-day or city-specific surcharges, and "airport concession fees" push the final bill up. Ask about these *before* arriving at the rental car counter.
- Although there is little you can do about it, be prepared to pay increasingly higher taxes. In an example of taxation without representation in its purest form, many city governments now milk car renters renting cars to pay for, among other things, sports arenas. Expect to pay locally imposed taxes and fees in excess of 20 percent in Chicago, Denver, Las Vegas, Minneapolis, Orlando, Phoenix, and Tampa. Remember that reservationists will not include additional taxes and fees in their quotes unless you ask.
- Airport locations saddled with too many cars may offer airport-only deals. You'll see signs posted at airport car rental counters offering these deals. Also, when you see "Cars Available" signs at the rental counter, forget about your reservation. Walk up to a few counters and negotiate the best rate possible.
- Check the Web. Hertz and Avis offer special weekend rates on their sites at www.hertz.com and www.avis.com. Also check Alamo's site at www.goalamo.com.

- In the late fall, car rental companies eager to build their inventories in Sun Belt cities will offer amazingly low drop-off rates (as low as $9.95 per day). Cars must be picked up in certain northern cities and dropped off in certain southern cities. Call and inquire about such plans in September or October. (The reverse is true in the spring when it's time to move the fleet back north.)

81—AT THE CAR RENTAL COUNTER

- How do you get the best car? Ask for the car with the least mileage. The counter agent has mileage information on his or her computer screen.
- You don't have to take the car that the agent chooses for you. This is especially true for weekly or extended rentals. Check out your car before you drive it off the lot. If you are dissatisfied, ask for another one. If you don't like the smell of smoke, request a nonsmoking car.
- According to industry convention, car rental agencies cannot downgrade you if they do not have a car of the size you reserved. They must upgrade you at no additional cost, and if they don't have any larger cars, they should send you to a competitor and pay any difference in the rate applied.
- Most car rental companies have more large cars than small ones. Reserve a compact car at a cheap rate—the

chances are that when you arrive and a compact is not available, you'll be upgraded to a larger car, free of charge.

- Always mention your affiliation with organizations such as American Automobile Association or other motor clubs, the American Small Business Association, the National Association for the Self-Employed, the American Association of Retired Persons, the Red Cross, or others for automatic discounts of 10 percent or more.
- For cheaper rates, check with off-airport, or local operators. Car rental companies that don't have to pay stiff airport taxes and fees for on-airport sites can afford to charge you less. *Important point:* Be sure you have directions on how to get back to the lot to return the car; many off-airport lots are very difficult to find, and are usually in desolate, if not dangerous, neighborhoods.
- *Warning:* New software programs allow car rental companies to access a growing number of state Department of Motor Vehicle records. You could be denied a car rental (at the counter, not when you make your reservation) if your license has been suspended or if your driving record shows that within the last three years you have been charged with driving under the influence of alcohol or drugs, reckless driving that resulted in bodily injury or property damage, involvement in two or more accidents, driving without proof of insurance, or

failing to report an accident. Rules for checking vary from state to state, so if you have a tarnished record, find out whether the car rental company will rent you a car *before* you arrive at the car rental counter with your boss or client!

- Don't fall for the counter agent's hard sell on different "refueling options." The most preposterous? "Pre-purchase a tank of gas and bring the car back empty!" Driving around a strange city on a low tank of gas? No, thanks. Be safe and save money by allotting enough time to stop and fill up the car yourself before returning it.
- If you will be late picking up your car, call the car rental company if possible. It will usually hold the car you have requested for only an hour after your scheduled arrival. If you don't make your scheduled arrival time, you may be forced to pay for a larger car or find no car at all.
- If you are tired of the car rental hard sell at the counter, sign up for "preferred" or "express" programs like Hertz No. 1 Gold or National's Emerald Aisle. This way, you only have to answer all the questions once a year when your membership is renewed. When you arrive at the counter, you present an ID, sign your contract, and you're off. They also offer upgrades and other perks.

82—UNDERSTAND INSURANCE ISSUES

- By now, most business travelers "just say no" to overpriced collision insurance ($7 to $20 per day), which is normally covered by the renter's personal auto insurance policy, the credit card used to pay for the car, or your company's policy. If you rely on your personal coverage, remember to check with your insurance company at least once a year to determine the validity of collision protection.
- If you *do not* own a car, it is important to review your liability protection. Recently, car rental companies quietly stopped protecting renters' liability. That means if you are in an accident that causes a loss of life or personal injury, you can be sued for damages. Most car owners are covered by their personal auto policies; however, those who do not own cars might opt for this protection. (About $15 per day.)
- Ask your credit card company if it provides *primary* or *secondary* coverage. Secondary coverage protects you only if your personal policy does not. The problem with secondary coverage is that in many cases, you may still be responsible for the deductible amount on your personal insurance. And since any accident will be reported to your insurance company, you can expect a rate increase.
- In some states, if you are pulled over by police, you must be able to prove that

the car has insurance. While this information is usually included in the car rental agreement, it's also mounted on a sticker underneath the trunk hood in many rental cars.

83—DRIVING TIPS

- Invest in a cellular phone (or rent one if you are renting a car). Some car rental companies will give you a phone; you only pay for the calls you make. A recent Gallup study found that people who use cell phones find travel less stressful. A cell phone is an excellent safety feature, and calls to 911 are usually free.
- Make driving a learning experience. Listen to books on cassette when on road trips. Popular topics include self-help, fiction, and business. Tapes cost $10 to $15 at most bookstores and record stores. Also, your friendly neighborhood video rental store may have books on tape that you can rent.
- Don't rent a car if you are only going to drive to your hotel and park. Consider your options: a free hotel shuttle, cab, limo, or public transportation. If you are renting only for short trips, ask about an hourly rate or one with a mileage cap of 100 or so miles per day.
- Hire a driver. Local college kids eager for extra cash or a retired executive looking for something to do make great drivers. Pay them $50 to $100 per day to drive

you to nearby cities while you work in the car: it's cheaper than flying and you'll get some work done. Ask for a receipt from the driver for services rendered so you can write the expense off or get reimbursed by your company.

- In 1998, the official IRS-approved per-mile driving rate was 32.5 cents. That is the amount you can deduct from your taxes for the miles you logged on business. The 32.5 cent standard (revised yearly) includes the cost of insurance, license and registration, depreciation, fuel, oil, tires, and maintenance.
- If you spend any time at all on the road, your office is the front seat of your car. Products like the AutoExec Pro, usually advertised in in-flight magazines, are molded plastic bins that work like desks and are secured in the passenger seat with the seat belt. They provide a large flat work space for writing or for a laptop and a storage compartment underneath for files, cell phone, and even a bubble-jet printer. (Mobile Office Environments, $179.95; tel: 800-373-9635) If you don't opt for something like this, always have a notepad or a small tape recorder nearby for unexpected brainstorms. But be careful—don't try to work and drive at the same time!
- Although driving is generally less expensive than flying, don't be misled into thinking that filling up the tank with gas will be the only cost incurred on a road

trip. According to consulting firm Runzheimer International, gas, maintenance, and tires only comprise about a fifth of the cost—11 cents per mile—of owning a 1997 Ford Taurus, for example. The bulk of the cost comes in ownership; insurance, registration, taxes, financing and depreciation which push the per-mile cost up another 34 to 45 cents. So that 400-mile road trip can actually cost $180.

84—INTERNATIONAL DRIVING

- U.S. drivers' licenses are valid in many countries. If you aren't sure, call the American Automobile Association (AAA), which can issue international driving permits.
- Inquire about the type of car you will be renting: many foreign locations rent only cars with manual transmissions. To determine coverage, check with your insurance company or credit card company before you go.

85—READ UP ON THE SUBJECT

Don't know the difference between a gasket and a fuel pump? If so, then check out the Nutz and Boltz Automotive Survival Guide by master mechanic David Solomon (Contemporary Books, $14.95). An automotive technician since 1964, he assists thousands of automobile owners through his weekly radio show and his newsletter, both titled *Nutz and Boltz.* Here are a few of his top tips for business travelers.

- "Cell phones may not be the best idea for road warriors—when you are out in the middle of nowhere a cell phone does you no good," he says. Instead, he suggests a relic of the 1970s, the CB radio, for those that spend a lot of time on lonesome highways. "Truckers still use CB radios a lot. They are excellent tools for determining road conditions ahead, avoiding speed traps, and getting emergency help," says Solomon. You can still buy CB radios at electronics and stereo stores for as little as $50.
- Seeking decent road food? A sign of a good roadside restaurant is a lot of trucks in the parking lot. "Truckers know where to find good food on the road," he says. Look for signs that say Homemade Pies or Home Cooking and avoid places with liquor or beer signs. That means that they are making money on booze, not good food.
- If your brakes fail, gently steer into and brush against the nearest guardrail, wall, or curb. The friction of the car against the object will slow you down, "It means body work later, but it's better than a fatal crash," says Solomon.
- "Buy the best tires you can afford," he says. "When the time comes that you need good tires, it's worth the cost. Tires make more difference than anything

does on your car. I recommend spending at least $400 for a good set."

86—HOW TO AVOID SPEEDING TICKETS

Here are some tips from the National Motorists Association on how to avoid speeding tickets.

- Don't stand out or move faster than surrounding traffic, weave, or cut across lanes. Avoid the left lane, if possible. Remember, it's the "fast" lane.
- Watch the trucks. If they are maintaining the posted speed limit, something is amiss and you should be wary.
- If you do get pulled over, don't insert Sir or Ma'am after every word. Police call that bootlicking and don't like it. Calling the officer by his or her rank (Lieutenant, Deputy, etc.) is good if used sparingly, but only use this tactic if you are absolutely sure of the officer's rank or title.
- Keep your car neat and clean. Papers, maps, and fast-food wrappers do not impress an officer looking in the windows.
- Stickers for the Police Benevolent Association or similar organizations don't work. The police know that the only people who have them are those trying to avoid tickets!
- For more information on the National Motorists Association, see www.motorists.com or call 608-849-6000.

87—PARKING LOT POINTERS

Large, dark parking lots are almost unavoidable during the course of a business trip. But there are ways a smart business traveler can avoid problems.

- *Airport parking:* Most major U.S. airports now have several private off-airport parking lots to accommodate overflow from the main on-airport lots. The best thing about these private lots is that they offer shuttle services that pick you up and drop you off at your car.
- *Rental car lots:* Most large car rental companies now provide their preferred customers with premium extras like van-to-car service.
- *Hotel parking lots:* Many large downtown hotels offer valet parking. Use it. However, if you are staying at a hotel without valet services, ask for an escort to your car. When arriving at a hotel without valet parking, ask for a hotel employee to ride with you to the parking lot and walk back with you.

88—PLAY IT SAFE ON THE ROAD

- *Driving is 70 to 100 percent more dangerous than flying.* Some airlines like to remind you of this in their landing announcements. ("Now that the safest part of your journey is over . . .") More Americans die each year in car accidents than died in Vietnam during a decade of U.S involvement.

- *Carry a spare tire and check it periodically.* Newer American cars have those hard-rubber tiny replacement tires to use when you have a flat. Older cars, and some European and Japanese models still have inflatable spares. Be sure that it is inflated.
- *Carry a roadside emergency kit.* These typically include basic tools, flares, a flashlight, blankets, jumper cables, and some first aid supplies. They can be real lifesavers.
- *Prepare for bad weather.* Check all fluid levels, tire pressure, spare tire, wiper blades, snow brush and ice scraper, and especially your car battery *before* you leave home or the car rental lot. And, remember that driving in snow, ice, rain, and fog requires special techniques. If you are not used to driving in winter weather, get advice from someone who is.
- *Carry an up-to-date map, and ask for directions before leaving the rental car lot.* Always request a map at the counter. And always get good directions to your hotel from the airport. Most crimes directed at drivers happen to those who are lost. Ask rental agents which areas of town to avoid.
- *Always keep your rental car locked—* even if you don't have anything in the main part of the car. You may think your valuables are protected in the trunk, but most cars today have a trunk release

somewhere in the car. If you don't lock the car, a thief can get in the trunk as easily as getting in the door!

- *Avoid parking in unguarded lots*—especially if your rental car has out-of-state tags or other identifying features. These cars shout "trunk full of goodies" to thieves. A rash of crimes directed at cars with rental company markings has forced most companies to remove them in most states. Another good idea—don't rent an inexpensive hatchback model if you are planning on storing things in your car.

89—HOW TO AVOID CAR JACKING

Here are a few basic safety tips that you should learn to follow automatically.

- Keep your luggage and other valuables in the trunk and out of sight. Keep your purse or briefcase on the floor—never on the front passenger seat.
- Keep at least one car length between you and the car in front of you when stopping. This prevents you from being blocked in and unable to get away if car jackers drive up behind you.
- If another car bumps you, if someone yells, honks, or points at your car as if there was something wrong, or if a driver flashes his headlights at you, *do not stop*. Drive to the nearest well-lit, populated place, then investigate. (Another good time to use a car phone.)

- Don't pick up hitchhikers. Just like your mother told you.
- Don't use unofficial roads—especially in foreign countries.
- If you must hire a car, use only licensed taxis and establish routes and fares first.

CHAPTER 7

At the Hotel

A hotel stay is a key part of most business trips, and all business travelers have endured as many hotel stays as they have enjoyed. Some hotel stays are memorable, some you try to forget, and some just blend into that one big beige hotel experience in the back of your mind.

Over the past several years, new hotels have been cropping up rapidly all over the country. Many are limited-service hotels with rooms designed especially for business travelers providing a wealth of amenities like large work desks, free copies and faxes, gyms, and in-house ATMs.

With all the choices you have, how do you know which deal is truly the best and where you will get the most consistently good service? The answer to this question depends on many factors, such as the length of your stay, your location, and what class of hotel you're looking for. This chapter will attempt to clear up some of your confusion and get you the most bang for your buck.

90—GETTING THE BEST RATE

- You can almost always get a better deal by calling the hotel directly instead of a central 800 reservations line. Sometimes by simply asking, "Is this the lowest rate available?" you can net big savings. Hotels have caught on to the airlines' practice of "yield management," which means that a hotel room that is worth *X* today could be worth *Y* tomorrow. So if at first you don't succeed, keep trying.
- A generic corporate rate is not always the best deal. If your company does not have a special rate, ask for the rate of the company you are visiting (even if it is a prospective client). Many times the hotel's local sales office has set up a special private rate that only in-house reservationists are aware of. (However, desk clerks are more likely to upgrade a traveler on a corporate rate than a discount rate.)
- Ask for association discounts. Membership in the American Automobile Association (AAA), the American Association of Retired Persons (AARP), or other national organizations can sometimes net discounts.
- Try hotel consolidators, which purchase hotel room blocks at deep discounts, then pass part of those savings on to travelers who book through their ser-

vices. While there is usually not a charge for the service, you may be required to pay in advance with a credit card. Try the Hotel Reservations Network (800-964-6835 or www.180096hotel.com); or Quikbook (800-789-9887 or www.quikbook.com). Keep in mind that some hotels that sell their rooms to consolidators really *need* the business, so they might not be the latest, greatest hotels in town. Good idea: Get an independent opinion of the hotel before you book it.

- Many travel agents band together with others to obtain volume-based discounts from individual and chain hotels. Always ask your travel agent to find you a *preferred or a consortium* rate, which can save you from 20 to 40 percent.

91—NEGOTIATE THE BEST DEAL

- If you plan to stay at a specific hotel for an extended period, arrange a meeting with a member of the hotel sales staff to negotiate your own private rate. If you can't get a break on price, ask for room upgrades, free breakfasts, even shoeshines, valet services, or local transportation in the hotel shuttle. Shop around. Most hotels are eager to snare long-term business.
- If you will be working in your hotel room during the summer, don't forget to request a room away from the shrieks and squeals of the hotel pool area.

- Beware of hidden charges and taxes, which can be as high as 15 to 20 percent in some cities. Also check ahead of time on extras that can add up, like incoming fax charges, per-call telephone charges, or hefty parking fees when driving. Staying at a hotel that limits these add-ons can help save money.
- Inquire about a package price for business-class rooms (with amenities like oversized desks, free local calls and long-distance access, in-room fax, coffeemaker, newspaper, etc.). Sometimes the premium you must pay for these rooms is worth it, sometimes it's not. But overall, these are a welcome idea to the travelers who feel nickel-and-dimed to death at the check-out counter. Ask about these rooms when you make your reservation.

92—NO ROOM AT THE INN?

Desperate? If you are stuck in a strange city with no reservation and can't find a room, ask the desk clerk or manager about the possibility of placing a roll-away bed in a meeting room for the night. If available, use the hotel health club to shower. You can also ask for an out-of-service room that might have ripped carpeting or a broken door but is still a better option than hauling off to another hotel (or sleeping on a park bench!).

93—OR THE WRONG INN ALTOGETHER?

If there is more than one Marriott, Hilton, or Hyatt in the city where you are going, be sure you know which one you have a reservation at. Otherwise, you could be in for a *long* cab ride.

94—GET TO KNOW YOUR FRONT-DESK CLERK!

What exactly can friendly front-desk clerks do for you? For starters, they can usually get you in a room when the hotel is otherwise "sold out." For example, the presidential suite is not always booked and paid for at a presidential rate. If it were available in an otherwise sold-out situation, that's where a friendly clerk might put a loyal guest. And in that case, the guest would pay no more than the rate for a standard room.

Get specific. Don't walk up to the front desk and demand "an upgrade." They get that kind of request all the time. If you are specific, you may get what you want. For example, if you are going to need room to spread out your work, ask for a large room. Or ask for a room with a view if you are there on a special occasion. Other things to ask for: a specific bed type, a room close to or far from an elevator, a room with a fax machine, or a very quiet room.

If you spend a lot of time in a certain city, pick one hotel and stay there as much as possible. Get to know the people behind the counter; ask for the same desk clerk every time you check in or make a reservation. If you have not had the time to build a relationship with the front-desk staff, personally call or write a cordial note to the front-office manager in advance of your stay. Explain that you are very excited about the stay and want to have a good experience. When called on personally, the manager is going to make a mental note, or better yet, a note on your reservation, to ensure that you have a good stay—and that can make all the difference.

95—WHEN THINGS GO WRONG What to do when you arrive at your hotel after a long journey and the perky young desk clerk tells you that although you have a guaranteed reservation (evidenced by the reservation confirmation number you are holding in your hand), there are no rooms available? The hotels have caught on to the airlines' practice of overbooking, and in their lingo, when there is no room available, the guest is "walked." If this happens to you, ask for:

1. A free long-distance telephone call to notify office or family of your hotel change
2. Free transportation to a nearby comparable hotel
3. A free night at a nearby hotel of equal or better quality

Some hotels will also offer you free upgrade certificates, meals, or weekend vouchers. Remember that you must *ask* for these things; otherwise you may not get them.

You stand a better chance of not getting walked if you *guarantee* your reservation with a credit card, which puts the hotel under a contractual obligation to honor your reservation. (A simple "confirmed" reservation is a much more flimsy agreement because there is no money on the line.) On the other hand, you have to show up; otherwise you pay for one night's stay. Also, try to reconfirm your reservation early on the day of your arrival.

Warning: In high-occupancy cities like New York and San Francisco, many hotels are moving up the traditional 6 P.M. arrival deadline to as early as 4 P.M. Be sure to ask before you arrive late. If you are delayed for any reason, call the hotel and let them know—then guarantee your room for "late arrival."

96—BEWARE OF HOTEL FEES

Leave before you say you will at many hotels and you will pay a penalty of anywhere from $25 to $50. Also, if you cancel your reservation without at least three days' notice, some hotels may penalize you. (The old standard for cancellations was by 6 P.M. on the day of arrival.)

Taking their cue from airlines (which impose penalties for changes or cancellations), hotels say this is only fair because it is virtually impossible to resell your room on such short notice.

How can you get around these new fees? Easy. Throw your weight around a little. If you or your company does a lot a business with a certain hotel or hotel chain, be sure the check-out clerk or manager knows that. If you have a hotel frequent-guest card, flash it. When pressed, most hotels say they deal with these new fees on a "case-by-case basis."

97—DON'T OVERSTAY YOUR WELCOME

Do you know your rules regarding eviction when it comes to renting a hotel room? They differ greatly from the rights that tenants get when renting an apartment, say lawyers Steve Colwell and Ann Shulman, authors of *Trouble Free Travel.* In most states, the hotel issues a "revocable license to use the room," meaning that if you overstay your welcome, the hotel can simply pack your bags and change your locks. No formal eviction proceedings are necessary.

98—NEW YORK CITY Getting a room in the Big Apple—the top stop on many business travel itineraries—is getting harder and harder, especially during the late-fall convention season. The New York Convention and Visitors Bureau (NYCVB), obviously overwhelmed by the fact that getting a room in the Big Apple is more difficult than ever, has released the following tips:

- Try the peak-season hotline at 800-846-ROOM. This service provides access to over 80 hotels in all price categories throughout the busy fall and holiday seasons. The NYCVB says that in 1997, on the 64 nights that travel agents and consumers thought the city was "sold out," the service was able to find rooms.
- Call independent or boutique hotels directly. (You'll find these in guidebooks or magazine articles.) They often have more rooms available as they are less well known and don't have toll-free numbers or the money to advertise.
- Use a travel agency. They have the resources and expertise to get bookings fast, especially on short notice during high-occupancy periods.
- This is risky, but it works: Call hotels just after 6 P.M. on the day you want to

stay. Most hotels cancel reservations not guaranteed with a credit card at 6 P.M. on the day of arrival. These nonguaranteed reservations—called "timers" by hoteliers—can turn a hotel's No Vacancy sign into Rooms Available.

99—HOW TO USE THE HOTEL ROOM PHONE

- When you check in, *always* ask what the fee for calling card access is. If you plan to make several calls and the hotel charges a big fee, you may choose to stay elsewhere. If you have no alternatives, you can always use the pay phone in the hotel lobby.
- If you are making a series of long-distance calls, hit the pound (#) sign between calls (don't hang up) for a new dial tone. Per-call fees stack up when you hang up and reenter your credit card number over and over.
- Complain to the hotel manager about the fees. If they are particularly outrageous, ask that they be removed from your bill when you check out.

100—COMMENTS, PLEASE

Hotels listen to customers who have significant comments, positive *or* negative, so go ahead and fill out that comment card if you have a chance. Business travelers account for up to 70 percent of all hotel guests. It is up to you to let hoteliers know how they are doing.

101—UNDERSTAND HOW THE HOTEL INDUSTRY IS ORGANIZED

Over the last decade, the hotel industry has become more and more segmented. It is important for business travelers to know what each segment means and where they fit in. Some major hotel chains like Marriott or Holiday Inn offer a hotel product in almost every segment. Others, like Four Seasons or Budgetel, specialize in a single segment. Here's a look at what you can expect in each segment.

Luxury Hotels

Luxury hotels cater to those looking for personalized services, fine dining restaurants, in-room business services, 24-hour room service, and posh fitness centers or spas. Special privileges and pampering make these hotels unique. Luxury chains with a major presence in the United States include Four Seasons, Ritz-Carlton, Grand or Park Hyatt, and the Sheraton Luxury Collection. Several independent hotels, resorts, and smaller chains affiliated with marketing groups like Preferred Hotels, Leading Hotels of the World, or Relais and Chateaux also fall into the luxury category. Typical guests include high-ranking corporate officers, successful entrepreneurs, and the independently wealthy.

Upscale Hotels

Upscale, or "quality," hotels have a diverse clientele ranging from conventioneers and business travelers to vacationing families. These full-service hotels are popular with business travelers because of their central (usually downtown or airport) locations and services and amenities like frequent-stay programs, meeting space, room service, business centers, express check-in and check-out, and fitness clubs. These hotels usually have concierge levels that offer luxury hotel services—typically a lounge offering free breakfasts and cocktail hours and a separate check-in area. Guests traveling on business are mostly mid- to upper-level managers and salespeople, incentive groups, and conventions. Chains include Swissotel, Inter-Continental, Westin, Renaissance, Nikko, Omni, Hilton, Hyatt, Sheraton, and Marriott.

Moderate Hotels

Business travelers concerned with cost and convenience use moderate hotels. Most offer a good location, on-site or nearby food and beverage options, meeting space, video in-room check-out, and sometimes exercise rooms. Because the services offered by these hotels can range from just under luxury hotel standards to just above economy hotel standards, it is a good idea to find out about the hotel before making a long-term reservation. Holiday Inn, Radisson, Ramada Inn, Days Inn, Howard Johnson, Hampton Inn, and Marriott Courtyard are some examples.

Economy or Budget Hotels

These limited-service hotels are attractive to independent business travelers, those on a per diem, or corporations geared to reducing travel budgets. Most offer few amenities but clean, comfortable rooms. It pays to seek out newer properties: inexpensive hotel rooms tend to show their age faster than pricier palaces, so ask how old the property is when you make your reservation. Before you leave home, ask the client you are going to visit if he knows of any new hotels near his site. Or if you pull off the interstate and are faced with a choice between an older, established-looking property or one that still has hay in the freshly landscaped lawn, go with the hay! Most budget properties do not have a restaurant on the premises, but you'll find many sharing a parking lot (and a symbiotic relationship) with a family-style or fern-bar type restaurant (like Bennigans, TGI Fridays). Chains include Budgetel, Marriott Fairfield Inns, Red Roof, Comfort Inns, La Quinta, Microtel, Holiday Inn Express, Days Inn, and Econo-Lodge.

Extended-Stay Hotels

Extended-stay "suite" hotels are most popular with people relocating to a new city, attending a training program, or on a temporary assignment. The homelike features of properties at the top end of this segment include kitchens, fireplaces, shopping services, complimentary breakfast, and weekly guest gatherings. However, many of the newer extended-stay properties are relatively sterile, providing only the bare minimum in services, and are usually located in the suburbs. Rates depend on how long the guest stays; most decrease significantly after the first 7 to 10 days. Full-service chains include Residence Inn by Marriott, Summerfield Suites, and Homewood Suites. While chains like Embassy Suites and Doubletree Suites offer two-room suites, most do not have kitchen facilities; instead, they offer free breakfast and afternoon snacks. Chains with fewer frills include Marriott's TownePlace Suites, Extended Stay America, and Suburban Lodges.

102—GET OUT OF THE MAINSTREAM

Increasingly popular alternatives to impersonal, run-of-the-mill hotels in all categories are lesser-known boutique hotels such as the Kimpton chain on the West Coast, or the Gotham Group or Manhattan East Suite Hotels in New York City.

With more personalized service and a more secure atmosphere, many business travelers have become bed-and-breakfast regulars. Ask about these finds by calling local chambers of commerce, convention and visitor's bureaus, or by word of mouth. There are also plenty of B and B directories on the Internet.

Here's an alternative to staying in a hotel for an extended period: Many apartment complexes will now rent by the night, with only a two- or three-night minimum. These furnished apartments, sometimes called *apartels,* are often cozier than hotel rooms and eliminate the process of checking in and out, paying inflated phone charges, and puzzling over bills—and a comfortable apartment is about half the price of a quality hotel. Apartels can be found in major cities around the United States, such as Atlanta, Boston, Chicago, Miami, New Orleans, New York City, Philadelphia, San Francisco, and Washington, D.C. Ask your travel agent how to find them.

103—LEARN ABOUT HOTELS CATERING TO SPECIAL NEEDS

- Marriott's popular Room That Works includes an oversized desk with power and phone jacks conveniently mounted on the desktop, as well as an ergonomically correct chair and a bright task light. Marriott has installed these conveniences in 3000 rooms nationwide, so ask for one next time you check in. There is no extra charge.

- Are you an insomniac? Hilton's Sleep Tight rooms offer a minibar stocked with bedtime treats like cookies and milk, cheese and crackers, and chamomile tea. Soundscape machines soothe with white noise, and you'll even find a face mask and ear plugs. If they could only have someone come by and sing lullabies! Available at Hiltons in many major cities—inquire when making your reservation.

104—TO GET A DEAL, STAY IN THE SUBURBS

With downtown or central-city hotel rates inching toward the sky, even those business travelers with meetings downtown are heading to the suburbs to sleep. Trading down to a less-expensive property on the edge of town may not be as bad as you think. Most of these hotels now actively court budget-minded business travelers with special amenities and rates. As a matter of fact, a nice new budget hotel in the suburbs could easily beat a high-priced, central-city competitor—at about half the price! So on your next business trip, forget the hassles and high prices of big downtown hotels. Leave those to the name tag-clad conventioneers. Go ahead and try one of these new suburban hotels, where small is beautiful and less really can be more. Here's a guide to help you better understand what to expect from the hotels growing fastest in the suburbs.

Midpriced Accommodations

Courtyard by Marriott: Distinguishing feature: Grandaddy of them all, consistent quality globally. Number of properties: 300 nationwide and in the UK. Reservations: 800-321-2211. Web site: www.courtyard.com. Average rate: $60 to $90

Hampton Inns: Distinguishing feature: 100 percent satisfaction guarantee—if for any reason you are dissatisfied with your stay, your money is refunded with no questions asked. Number of properties: 650 nationwide and in Canada, Thailand, Costa Rica, and Chile. Reservations: 800-426-7866. Web site: www.hampton-inn.com. Average rate: $61

La Quinta Inns: Distinguishing feature: Every single room was renovated in 1997. Number of properties: 250, mostly in Sun Belt states. Reservations: 800-687-6667. Web site: www.laquinta.com. Average rate: $60

Wingate Inns: Distinguishing feature: All new from-the-ground-up in 1997, lounge chairs, cordless phones. Number of properties: 50+ nationwide. Reservations: 800-228-1000. Web site: www.wingateinns.com. Average rate: $80

Economy Hotels

Budgetel or Baymont: Distinguishing feature: 100 percent offer BusinessFirst rooms; continental breakfast delivered to room. Number of properties: 145 in 30 states, mostly in the midwest and southeast. Reservations: 800-428-3438. Web site: www.budgetel.com. Average rate: $50

Days Inn Business Place: Distinguishing feature: Free snack at check-in, in-room microfridge. Number of properties: 150+ nationwide. Reservations: 800-329-7466. Web site: www.daysinn.com. Average rate: $55

Fairfield Inn by Marriott: Distinguishing feature: Ubiquity and Marriott consistency. Number of properties: 300 nationwide. Reservations: 800-228-2800. Web site: www.fairfieldinn.com. Average rate: $55

Holiday Inn Express: Distinguishing feature: Large, full-service guest room and free continental breakfast bar. Number of properties: 570 worldwide. Reservations: 800-465-4329. Web site: www.holiday-inn.com. Average rate: $60

Microtel: Distinguishing feature: All properties are brand new from the ground up in 1997. Number of properties: 50+, mainly in the southeast and midwest. Reservations: 888-771-7171. Web site: www.microtelinn.com. Average rate: $42

Red Roof: Distinguishing feature: Business King rooms with king-size bed, desk; some with recliners. Number of properties: 249, mostly in the eastern United States. Reservations: 800-843-7663. Web site: www.redroof.com. Average rate: $45

Sleep Inn: Distinguishing feature: A 73-inch-longdesk and an oversized shower. Number of properties: 125 worldwide. Reservations: 800-627-5337. Web site: www.sleepinn.com. Average rate: $50

105—CHECK OUT THE HOTEL LOCATION BEFORE THE TRIP Ask your travel agent or someone from the city where you are going about the hotel's neighborhood. If you are in a questionable area, ask a hotel employee to park your car for you. Also, the hotel should provide escorts to the parking lots upon request. If you are an exercise buff, ask about the safest areas to jog or run. When on the road, try to run in the morning or at lunch; avoid outdoor workouts if it is dark.

106—KNOW FIRE ESCAPE AND SURVIVAL PROCEDURES Just like air crash survivors, hotel fire survivors report that they had their escape route mapped out *before* the fire alarm went off. Just take a quick look at the diagram on the back of your door. *In case of a fire:* If there is no fire in the hallway, head to the exit, taking your room key. If you sense heat and smoke, stay low. If stuck in your room, fill the bathtub with water, soak towels, call the front desk to report the fire and your whereabouts. To help fire fighters locate you, open or remove the drapes from your window, write HELP on the glass using shaving cream, soap, or whatever is available. Breathe through a moistened washcloth.

107—PLAY IT SAFE IN YOUR HOTEL

- Use hotel safes for your valuables. Don't try to hide valuables in your room. An experienced burglar will find any hiding place you create. Store jewelry, cash, and electronic or other valuables in an in-room safe or hotel safe deposit box. Better yet, don't bring them along in the first place.
- Stay on the third through the sixth floor. Burglars are more likely to target rooms on the lower levels, and fire-fighting equipment doesn't always reach above the sixth.
- Hang up the Do Not Disturb sign and leave the TV on when you go out. Never leave the Maid Please sign on the door. Call housekeeping and ask to have your room cleaned instead.
- Always verify room deliveries. Check with the front desk or room service when an unannounced delivery arrives at your door.

108—FIND OUT BEFORE YOU ARRIVE

When you are making your reservation, ask whether the hotel has these basic safety features.

- *Well-lit interior hallways with monitored entrances*: It is easier to secure rooms in hotels with one or two monitored entrances. Motels with exterior doors in unattended areas are prime targets.

- *Electronic door locks:* It's impossible to duplicate plastic or magnetic keys found in most hotels today.
- *24-hour security patrol and room service*: This will discourage you from leaving your room late at night for a midnight snack—but ensuring that if you do, someone is on the lookout for shady characters. Are there ATM cash machines in the hotel lobby?
- *Adequate locks and peepholes on hotel room doors*: Your door should have a dead bolt, a chain, and a regular door lock. Be sure all three are secure before going to bed. Some business travelers place the small brown rubber wedges that are designed to keep doors open behind the closed door to prevent forced entry.

Confessions of a Frequent Traveler: San Francisco

I always request a window seat for the flight to San Francisco. I like to look down and see the Mississippi, the Rockies, and the Sierra. Owing to recent drenching rains, flying into the Bay Area this time was like flying into Central America. Instead of what normally look like suede upholstered brown hills, I saw bright green meadows, sparkling lakes, and a very muddy San Francisco Bay. Remember during the drought when you couldn't even get a glass of water in a California restaurant without asking?

I always try to stay in a different hotel every time I go to San Francisco. The city has some of the most innovative and impressive hotels anywhere. Let's see, over the last few years, I've stayed at the Nikko, the Monaco, the Marriott, the Huntington, the Clift, the Chancellor, the Ritz-Carlton, the Park Hyatt, and the Pan-Pacific. This time, it was the Mandarin Oriental.

The Mandarin and the Ritz regularly vie for "top hotel in the city" status. Which one wins depends on the type of biz traveler you are. The Ritz is very much like other Ritz hotels around the country: comfy, familiar, employees reciting "my pleasure," in an old and historic building near Nob Hill.

The Mandarin, on the other hand, is sheer architecture, softened by Asian-style service. The hotel is located downtown in the top 10 floors of the First Interstate Tower (the building that looks like a tuning fork, with big flags on each pinnacle). Only 105 rooms soar almost 50 floors above the financial district. Floor-to-ceiling windows and bathtubs perched on the edge of oblivion make this as dramatic a hotel room as I've ever seen—but no place for acrophobes.

There's no better city for a business trip than San Francisco. When the weather is nice, I get up early (because my body is on East Coast time), get out and find a good strong cup of coffee and a bagel, and walk to my meetings. . . . Usually I take taxis to or from meetings, but on this trip I discovered the Muni, a modern version of streetcars that you see only in San Francisco proper. The better-known BART system is mostly used for transporting people long distances—like to or from the East Bay and Oakland. I liked the Muni—fares are only a dollar, and it beats high taxi fares.

Speaking of high cab fares—the $35 fare to and from the airport may soon be a thing of the past as BART is about to break ground on a new line that will run from the central city to the airport. But if it takes as long to put in a BART line as it did to repair the freeways after the 1989 Loma Prieta earthquake, it could be at least five years away. . . .

Pecking away on the laptop on the plane home. . . . These big old Delta L-1011s are creaky and shaky on takeoff—sometimes it feels like this old bird is going to fall apart as it lifts itself into the sky. . . . Will be glad when Delta finally buys a new wide-body and gets rid of these old "lead-sleds." That's what pilots call them, because of their weight and appetite for fuel. . . . Looking out the window at the dull old patched-up wing reminds me of Eastern Airlines in its dying days. . . .

CHAPTER 8

Using the Telephone

The telephone is without question the most used tool of the business traveler. But rapidly advancing technology combined with deregulation conspire to make a simple long-distance call confusing to many. And in the last few years, new ways to stay in touch have popped up like mushrooms. These days communications options include the phone, e-mail, pagers, cell phones, voice mail, in-flight phones, and faxes. Here are some ways to be sure that you are getting the biggest bang for your telephone bucks.

109—DEALING WITH HOTEL PHONES

Typically, a traveling salesperson must make a series of long-distance calls each night to report back on the day's activity, to call a boss or coworker, to set up future appointments, or to call home. Fees for accessing long-distance carriers from hotel room phones vary widely, from free to $1.50. Fees are no problem when the traveler makes one or two calls a night. But when you make several calls over the course of a trip, these charges can really stack up.

- *Avoid toll-free access charges.* Because of outcries from frustrated business travelers, as well as competitive pressures, most major hotel chains have stopped charging fees for calls to 800/888 numbers. However, not *all* of them have done so. This inconsistency is mostly because of the way hotels are owned. If the hotel is a corporate-owned property, no-fee-for-long-distance-access policies are easy to enforce. However, many hotels are independent franchises, and some owners don't see the benefit in eliminating such fees. Many nonchain boutique hotels and resorts are the worse offenders when it comes to 800/888 access fees. So *always ask* about these fees when you make your reservation.
- *Always ask about calling card access fees when you check in, too.* If you plan to make a large number of calls, you may choose to stay elsewhere. If worse comes to worse, use the pay phone in the hotel lobby. (In some cases, you may find it cheaper to use your cell phone.) If you are stuck with a bill that you feel is unfair, complain to the manager. Request that it be reduced or eliminated.
- *Don't dial direct.* Always use a credit card when making long-distance calls.

Direct-dialed calls from your room are typically assessed at a 40 percent premium (higher outside the United States). To avoid outrageous surcharges for using your hotel room phone, access your long-distance carrier directly by dialing one of the following numbers:

AT&T: 1-0-2-8-8-0 or 800-CALL-ATT

MCI: 1-0-2-2-2-0 or 800-888-8000

Sprint: 1-0-3-3-3-0 or 800-877-8000

Note: Sometimes by using the shorter 1-0--- number you can get around a hotel's fee for calls to "800" numbers.

- *Know where to complain.* Federal Communications Commission (FCC) rules require hotels and pay phones to allow access to all long-distance carriers. If you are prevented from making calls via the carrier of your choice, or if you feel gouged, report it to the FCC Enforcement Division, Common Carrier Bureau, 2025 M Street, Washington, DC 20554.
- *Hit #.* When making a series of credit card calls, don't hang up between calls. Hit the pound sign (#) between calls (at hotels that allow it) to avoid an individual fee for each call. Fees stack up when you enter your credit card number over and over.
- *Schedule your calls.* To save time and money and preserve your peace of mind, set up a telephone call schedule with your office and with your family. For example, let your office know that you will call in for messages every day at

1:15 P.M. Arrange to call your family every Tuesday and Thursday at 7 P.M. That way, you won't waste time and money leaving messages.

110—GET THE BEST DEAL IN CALLING CARDS

For business travelers, long-distance charges add up to hundreds, if not thousands, of dollars each year. To get the best value, shop around and switch carriers to take advantage of the constantly changing rates.

- *Avoid surcharges:* Did you know that every time you make a calling card call with most major carriers, you are charged a 30 to 80 cent surcharge in addition to toll charges? The largest carriers play a game of cat and mouse with these surcharges—some charge them, some don't—depending on the plan you choose. And once you agree to a "surcharge-free" plan, some carriers are known to go back on their promise and quietly begin to assess the surcharge again. Therefore, it's not only important to make the best decision the first time around: be sure to check up on your plan each year. If the rules have changed, switch.
- *Stand-alone cards:* You can shop around for the best stand-alone long-distance calling card—and not have to switch your basic home or business long-distance carrier to do so. (Suggestions: Premiere, 800-609-2030; Voicenet, 800-864-2363; Frontier, 800-783-2020)

- *Coding calls:* With some (not all) calling cards, you can assign an accounting code to each call, making reimbursement from multiple clients much easier. Ask about this feature when you sign up. It is usually free.
- *Prepaid calling cards:* One new trend to sweep the long-distance telephone market: prepaid or *debit,* calling cards. You buy a debit card with a specific dollar value (i.e., $10, $25, $50), call the toll-free number listed on the card, enter a PIN code, and make calls nationwide or worldwide at a flat rate. When the time is used up, you throw the card away. Debit cards are good for limiting your exposure if the card number is stolen; giving a set amount of long distance to traveling employees, college students, colleagues, customers, or friends; giving as a premium to customers or potential clients. Until recently, their biggest drawback has been cost, but with the AT&T, MCI, Sprint, grocery stores, and thousands of other vendors jumping in the market, charges have tumbled to less than 25 cents per minute. Charges vary greatly, however, so *ask.*
- *New features:* Traditional calling cards are getting a makeover. New "enhanced" calling cards are different from the standard-issue cards in that they offer a wider range of features. Most offer extras like voice and fax mailboxes, instant conference calling, news, sports, weather, stock and soap opera updates,

and horoscopes. Some even have optical scanning devices that can "read" your e-mail messages or faxes.

- *Watch out for "usage fees":* When you call your long-distance carrier's 800/888 number from a *pay phone,* it isn't free. Even though you aren't dropping any coins into that phone, as you enter your calling card number and make a call, your account could be billed an extra 30 cents. An FCC ruling that went into effect in late 1997 allows the owners of pay phones to assess a 28.4 cent "usage fee" on the recipients of 800 number calls. That means that the pay phone owner now charges AT&T, MCI, Sprint (and others) when you access their long-distance networks via an 800/888 number. And most long-distance companies are simply passing that fee on to you in the form of a 30-cent surcharge. (That's in addition to the standard calling card surcharge you are paying.) One way to avoid these fees is to use your cell phone instead of a pay phone. It sounds crazy, but with increasing surcharges, the cost of a credit card call is approaching that of a cellular call. Especially with cell phone rates dropping.

111—CELL PHONES: AT HOME . . .

Currently, about 1 in 10 Americans uses a cellular phone, and that number grows daily. To handle the growth, cellular phone companies are going digital. With a digital cell phone, you can expect better coverage in buildings, longer battery standby times, Web access, caller ID, enhanced paging services, and perhaps most importantly, better fraud protection. However, not all parts of the country offer digital service, an unfortunate fact that could render your newfangled phone obsolete during a business trip. *Best bet:* If you must have a spiffed-up digital phone with all the bells and whistles, compromise with a dual-mode analog-digital device.

112—AND ABROAD

The cell phone you use in the United States might not work abroad because cellular system radio frequencies vary from country to country. However, the SIM cards in new-generation digital phones can be swapped out for those wanting to roam in other countries. Ask your cellular provider for assistance before you leave. Another solution: just rent a cell phone from your hotel or car rental company when you arrive at your overseas destination.

113—UNDERSTAND IN-FLIGHT PHONES

- There are two players in the domestic in-flight phone business: GTE Airfone and AT&T Wireless. GTE Airfone controls a big chunk of the U.S. market, outfitting almost all Continental, America West, United, TWA, US Airways, and Delta aircraft. AT&T Wireless outfits American, Northwest, Southwest, and Alaska aircraft.
- Calls cost about $3 to set up, then another $2.50 or so per minute thereafter.
- On many aircraft, access to the Internet and e-mail are available from seatback

phones. However, poor connections tend to garble transmissions.

- Most in-flight phones can now receive calls from the ground. (So much for getting away from it all.) However, you don't have to answer these phones. GTE and AT&T have mercifully installed caller ID on incoming calls, so you only take calls that you want to.
- In-flight phones only work within 50 miles or so of the U.S. mainland. Many carriers with transoceanic service now offer phone service that uses satellites to transmit your calls, but the cost is truly prohibitive: around $7 to $10 per minute.

114—CONSIDER PERSONAL 800 SERVICES

The explosion of new technology and new phone service providers has brought the cost of 800/888 service down to the manageable level. You may want to consider personal 800/888 service if:

- You, your spouse, or your children frequently call home from out-of-town.
- You call your answering machine several times a day to check for messages.
- You stay at hotels that charge access fees for connection to long-distance services, but not to toll-free numbers.
- Your long-distance carrier charges "set-up" fees for every credit card call.

The personal 800/888 services of the major phone companies charge around $5 per month and 20 to 25 cents per call. Service set-up fees range from nothing to $10. Smaller telecommunications companies and resellers offer even better packages. *Important points:* 800/888 service runs through your existing phone lines. And you don't have to change your current long-distance carrier to get the 800/888 service from another carrier.

115—PAY LESS FOR INTERNATIONAL CALLING

- *Local-access numbers:* Sometimes outrageous international hotel surcharges and local taxes can add up to more than the cost of the call itself. If you know that you will be making a lot of long-distance calls on a trip overseas, call your carrier before you go and ask about local-access numbers in the country where you're going. (Also check the wallet-sized cards provided or see the ubiquitous ads in international editions of U.S. periodicals.) Once outside North America, you simply dial your carrier's local-access number (usually toll-free) from any phone in the country, which connects you automatically to your long-distance network in the United States. At that point, you either enter your calling card number or access an operator for calls back to the United States or to most other countries. Country-to-country calling can be limited with some cards—best to check ahead of time. Charges appear on your home or office phone bill, not your hotel bill.
- *More hidden charges:* Prior to the days of international calling cards, hotels

catering to American business travelers made a killing by overcharging hotel guests for international calls. The advent of new international calling cards means that hoteliers no longer have that profit center. To recoup, many program their phone systems to recognize calls to long-distance-carrier access numbers—and charge a hefty premium in some cases.

- *Cheaper service providers:* You might be paying much more than you should when calling home from overseas. A 1998 *Consumer Reports Travel Letter* survey found that the big three—AT&T, MCI, and Sprint—all charge close to $5 for a three-minute call from the UK to the United States, while smaller carriers like VoiceNet or Premiere Worldlink charge less than half that much.
- *Debit cards abroad:* If you plan to make a lot of local or domestic long-distance calls from public phones while in another country, consider buying a phone debit card from a post office or newsstand. This way, you just insert the card into a public phone and dial away instead of fumbling through your pockets for unfamiliar foreign coins.
- *Touch-tone generators:* Many countries outside North America do not have touch-tone systems, but many U.S.-based travelers' answering machines and voice mail systems require tones to retrieve messages. *Solution:* Electronics stores like Radio Shack provide "tone generators," pocket-sized gadgets that emit a tone into the phone mouthpiece.

Confessions of a Frequent Traveler: An Urban Myth Worth Dispelling

Among the hyper-connected business travel set, urban myths make the rounds in a fraction of the time they used to. Here's a shockingly believable story I heard long before we were all on e-mail. Now it falls into my e-mail box at least once a year. Here's how it goes. . . .

Version A:

A business traveler went down to the hotel bar for a drink after a long day's work. He was having a good time, had a couple of beers and some girl seemed to like him and suggested they go back to his room for a drink. They went back to his room, had a drink and even partook in some illegal drugs.

The next thing he knew, he woke up completely naked in the hotel bathtub filled with ice. He was still feeling the effects of the drugs, but looked around to see he was alone. He looked down at his chest, which had "CALL 911 OR YOU WILL DIE" written on it in lipstick. He saw a phone was on a stand next to the tub, so he picked it up and dialed. He explained what the situation was to the EMS operator and that he didn't know where he was, what he took, or why he was calling. She advised him to get out of the tub. He did, and she asked him to look himself over in the mirror. He did, and appeared normal, so she told him to check his back. He did, only to find two 9 inch slits on his lower back. She told him to get back in the tub immediately, and they sent a rescue team over. Apparently, after being examined, he found out more of what had happened. His kidneys were stolen. They are worth $10,000 each on the black market. Regardless, he is currently in the hospital on life support, awaiting a spare kidney. The University of Texas in conjunction with Baylor University Medical Center is conducting tissue research to match the victim with a donor.

Version B:

I wish to warn you about a new crime ring that is targeting business travelers. This ring is well organized, well funded, has very skilled personnel, and is currently in most major cities and recently very active in New Orleans.

The crime begins when a business traveler goes to a lounge for a drink at the end of the workday. A person in the bar walks up and offers to buy the traveler a drink. That's the last thing the traveler remembers until he wakes up in a hotel room bathtub, his body submerged to his neck in ice. There is a note taped to the wall instructing him not to move and to call 911. A phone is on a small table next to the bathtub for him to call. The business traveler calls 911 and is instructed by the 911 operator to very slowly and carefully reach behind him and feel if there is a tube protruding from his lower back. The business traveler finds the tube and answers, "Yes." The 911 operator tells him to remain still, having already sent paramedics to help. The operator knows that both of the business traveler's kidneys have been harvested. This is not a scam or out of a science fiction novel, it is real. It is documented and confirmable. If you travel or someone close to you travels, please be careful.

Sadly, this is very true. My husband is a Houston Firefighter/EMT and they have received alerts regarding this crime ring. It is to be taken very seriously. The daughter of a friend of a fellow firefighter had this happen to her. Skilled doctors are performing these crimes! Additionally, the military has received alerts regarding this. This story blew me away. I really want as many people to see this as possible so please bounce this to whoever you can. Is this not one of the scariest things you have ever heard of? PLEASE forward this to everyone you know.

The Truth

Press Release: The National Kidney Foundation Dispels Rumors About Illegally Harvested Kidneys

April 4, 1998, New York, NY—A persistent rumor that has been circulating for the past ten years has recently been reborn on the Internet: a business traveler has a drink with a stranger and wakes up in a tub full of ice, minus both kidneys.

The foundation has received calls from concerned business travelers who have been warned by their travel agents to beware of this 'crime ring' when traveling. "It's an urban myth run amok," says Dr. Wendy Brown, chairman of the National Kidney Foundation. "There is no evidence that such activity has ever occurred in the United States," says Dr. Brown.

Although this story is unfounded and untrue, many who hear it believe that this could really happen. "It is unfortunate when inaccurate information is reported about the organ donor process," states Dr. Brown. "In truth, transplanting a kidney from a living donor involves numerous tests for compatibility that must be performed before the kidney is removed. So it's highly unlikely that a gang could operate in secrecy to recover organs that would be viable for a transplant," Dr. Brown explains.

That much-traveled e-mail message gives specific details about incidents in New Orleans and Las Vegas, with embellishments by other Internet users that seem to give credence to the story, but none of the supposed victims is ever identified. In an effort to dispel this urban myth, the National Kidney Foundation is asking any individual who claims to have had his or her kidneys illegally removed to step forward and contact the foundation.

Dr. Brown is concerned that the unfortunate rumors will affect the public's willingness to become organ donors at a time when more than 50,000 Americans are awaiting life-saving organ transplants and 9 to 10 people on the waiting list die each day. She urges the public to call the National Kidney Foundation at 800-622-9010 for accurate information about the organ donor process and to receive a free organ donor card.

PART TWO

General Information

CHAPTER 9

Frequent Traveler Programs

There are three milestones in the history of airline industry. The first, of course, is the Orville and Wilbur Wright story. Second, the introduction of commercial jet aircraft in the 1960s. The third is no doubt the launch of frequent traveler programs in 1981. In the years since, this marketing phenomenon has become firmly entrenched in the travel industry, spreading beyond the airlines to hotel chains, car rental companies, cruise lines, and credit cards. In 1997, programs in the United States gave away almost 10 million frequent flier awards. And after years of looking down their noses at them, most international carriers now offer frequent traveler programs. So for better or for worse, it looks as though the programs are here to stay.

The appeal of frequent traveler programs is obvious: free travel; airline, hotel, and car upgrades; and more respect at the ticket counter, to name a few. But staying on top of each program, tracking your miles, sifting through endless statements, program newsletters, and advertisements, and even finding time to take the free trips are frustrations that all frequent travelers endure. Many of the major U.S. carriers are downsizing their fleets, buying smaller planes, and cutting back on flight frequencies. That means fewer seats, and even fewer "free" seats allotted for frequent travelers, making proper frequent travel program management all the more important.

As airlines continue to whittle away at benefits and focus on truly "frequent" customers, travelers must stay up-to-date to protect the miles they've built. Here are some tips to help you wade through this ever-growing, ever-changing milieu.

116—STAY UP TO DATE

Fierce competition for the loyalty of the business traveler has the airline programs offering a rapidly changing array of perks and promotions. Industrywide instability has program partners bowing in and bowing out at least yearly.

To the harried frequent traveler's rescue is Randy Petersen, perhaps the nation's most authoritative voice when it comes to these programs. Petersen is the owner of Colorado Springs–based Frequent Flyer Services (FFS), which offers several helpful tools to program members.

- It publishes *InsideFlyer,* a monthly magazine that tracks the programs and helps travelers stay on top of the ever-changing promotions, bonuses, awards, information, and advice ($36/year, tel: 800-767-8896).

- Many of Petersen's tips, as well as charts explaining over 50 frequent traveler programs are compiled in his annual *Official Frequent Flyer Guidebook* (AirPress, $14.99).
- To help frequent travelers maintain an accurate accounting of the points and credits accumulated in all their programs, FFS tracks individual programs for members. They also offer protection on members' mileage banks if an airline defaults. Information: 800-209-2870.
- If you're on-line, try www.webflyer.com. The mountain of information on this site is a basic download of the Petersen's encyclopedic knowledge. Here you will find news and candid advice on all programs, chat rooms to help sort out problems, hot links to all pertinent Web sites, and access to individual accounts in over a dozen programs.
- For those of you without Web access, Petersen's frequent flier empire also offers FlyerFax, a free fax-back service that contains hundreds of pages of information on most programs. Call 719-572-2700 for details.

117—CONCENTRATE ON ONE OR TWO PROGRAMS

Your most important goal should be to try to get into the *elite levels* of your programs. Entry into the elite means that the airlines will treat you as a true frequent flier—not just someone who has filled out a membership application. As an elite member, you get r-e-s-p-e-c-t.

You'll get mileage bonuses, easier access to upgrades, advance boarding privileges, better seats in coach, a larger carry-on allowance, private reservations numbers, limited blackouts, and other benefits.

- Flying on only one or two airlines will get you to the elite levels of membership much faster. Most airlines offer basic elite membership to those members who fly 25,000 miles per year.
- As airlines try to attract the true crème de la crème, elite levels are establishing new hierarchies. For example, Continental's OnePass program awards bronze, silver, and gold levels of elite membership. Delta's SkyMiles Medallion program offers silver, gold, and platinum levels.
- Periodically, some airlines will give "trial" elite status to members of other airline elite members. All you have to do is provide proof that you're an elite member of another program. Airlines normally don't publicize this, so you must call the airline's service center and ask.

118—WEIGH YOUR OPTIONS

In many cities, such as Pittsburgh, Atlanta, Houston, Dallas, Miami, Denver, and other "fortress hub" cities, your frequent flier program "decision" is moot. For those living in cities with more diverse choices or those in hub cities choosing a secondary airline, take these questions into consideration:

- Do you want free trips to international destinations? Some airlines have better international networks or program partners than others.
- Do you prefer to use your awards for upgrades? Some programs are much more liberal with upgrades than others.
- How about merchandise awards? For those who would rather not get on another plane to use their awards, some airlines offer better merchandise programs than others.
- Who will use your awards? Most airlines now allow members to transfer the awards to anyone they choose. It's okay to *give away* your miles—just don't get caught *selling* them.
- When do you plan to redeem your miles? Award time limits vary. Some airlines' miles expire after two or three years. Some don't.
- Who are the airline's partners? Proper management of partner hotel, car rental, long distance, and credit card programs can add 20 to 30 percent to your annual mileage bottom line.

119—END-OF-YEAR MILEAGE CRAMMING

Fliers earn elite status on most lines after flying 25,000 miles in a calendar year; higher tiers must fly 50,000 miles per year, and so on. And the cream of each program—under names like platinum, diamond, or premier—usually start at around 100,000 miles per year. The *only* way to get into airline elite levels is to get on a plane and fly, earning what are known as "base miles." Bonus miles earned from partners don't count toward elite status. As the end of each year approaches, smart travelers should employ last-minute strategies to get in under the rope.

Here are some ideas for topping off your mileage balance at the end of the year.

- *Take a cheap trip.* Look for short or less expensive flights on routes where major airlines compete with low-fare carriers. Most of these require 14 to 21 days advance purchase but no stayover requirement, so you can make a day trip of it if you'd like. If you've got nothing better to do on Christmas or New Year's, the even cheaper holiday-only fares are a good idea.
- Take a trip using an Internet weekend special. American's NetSaver fares or Continental's Cool Travel Specials offer rock-bottom rates *and miles* on these flights.
- *Increase your segments.* If you can't get into elite levels with your base miles, try getting in based on the number of segments you fly. Instead of flying nonstop, double your segment earnings by changing planes in airline hub cities on longer transcontinental trips.

120—BE A SMART REDEEMER—PLAN AHEAD

No matter how far in advance you'd like to take your free trip, *now* is the time to start planning for it. Free seats, sometimes already limited by blackout dates and heavy bookings, sell out fast, especially to the most popular destinations. For example, the tightest European summer destinations for most carriers are usually London and Paris. Domestically, flights usually fill up fast to hot spots in Florida (especially Orlando), California, and Hawaii, as well as cooler vacation cities in New England. During the winter, it's almost impossible to find seats, purchased *or* free, to warm-weather destinations like Hawaii, Florida, or the Caribbean.

Here are some tips to keep in mind when cashing in those hard-earned miles.

- First, remember that frequent flier miles are generally valued at about 2 cents per mile. That means that a 25,000 mile free domestic round trip is worth about $500. Keep that in mind when evaluating whether you want to purchase a ticket or redeem your miles. Save your frequent flier miles for upgrades, expensive transcontinental flights, or midweek trips. It's senseless to use valuable miles on tickets that you can buy for less than $200. (Consider that *before* you redeem miles for flights to cities where low-fare carriers keep fares low.)
- If you are going to redeem for a free round trip at the "cheapest" 25,000 mile level, decide on a *range* of departure and return dates before you call the airline—especially when redeeming for a trip during peak summer or winter vacations. *Tip:* First, call the airline to find out when you can fly. Then, ask your boss for the vacation days!

- If you are set on specific dates and require the luxury of no blackouts or capacity controls, you'll have to cough up the 40,000 or 50,000 miles required for a "standard" domestic award.
- If you are having trouble getting into a tight business travel market like New York or Los Angeles, try requesting flights on days that business travelers usually avoid like Tuesday, Wednesday, Thursday, or Saturday. Also, consider less popular times of day—forget Friday afternoons or Monday mornings! The two best months for free travel: October and May. The two worst: December and January.
- Try alternative airports. For example, if you can't get into Los Angeles International (LAX), try Long Beach, Orange County, Burbank, or Ontario. Can't get into Miami? Try Fort Lauderdale, West Palm Beach, or Fort Myers. And if all the seats to San Francisco International are taken, try Oakland, San Jose, Monterey, or even Sacramento. This works particularly well in Europe, where cities are relatively close and there's an excellent train system to get you to your city of choice. Can't get into London? Try Manchester, Brussels, or Amsterdam (here's your chance to try the Chunnel).
- Try alternate routing. If you can't get a nonstop flight to the city you desire, try a flight routed through another hub city.

- If the flights you want aren't available, ask to be wait-listed. Or call back. Plans change, flight inventories change, so a flight that's full this week could have an open seat next week or next month. Your best chances for finding an available free seat are far in advance—or at the last minute.

121—KEEP AN EYE ON YOUR ACCOUNT Always keep your boarding pass and passenger coupon portion of your ticket and match this with your frequent flier statement. If the credit does not show up, you'll need both pieces of paper to get credit. And keep a close eye on airline partners: some are notorious for *not* posting proper credit, or posting it late. Many programs now allow you to view your account status at their Web sites, and some, like www.biztravel.com, will keep a running tally of miles in several of your frequency program accounts.

122—USE YOUR POINTS TO UPGRADE The ability to upgrade is probably the most cherished benefit of frequent flier programs. There are three main avenues frequent fliers should use to move into the cozy confines of the first-class cabin.

- Cash in your miles for upgrade certificates to be used for confirmed first-class seats. Most airlines require about 20,000 miles to upgrade from coach to first class when traveling in the United States. These provide the most value when you are taking a long-haul transcontinental or international flight. International upgrades start at around 40,000 miles.

- Airlines usually mail out complimentary elite-level upgrade certificates (or deposit them into an electronic account) when your balance hits certain thresholds. These certificates offer elite members holding coach tickets the opportunity to upgrade to first class a few days before the flight (by calling in at a specified time) or on a space-available basis at the gate. Only the top-of-the-heap elite platinum or gold members are allowed to use these upgrades when making their reservations.
- For frequent travelers flying on certain fares, most airlines provide the opportunity to purchase an upgrade for significantly less than the price of a true first-class ticket. The price of the upgrade depends on the length of the flight. Still other airlines will confirm a first-class seat for members paying full-coach or unrestricted fares or members who are flying through certain hub cities.

123—BUILD MILEAGE BANKS USING PARTNER PROGRAMS

- You can substantially add to your total miles and points annually by properly choosing and using the airlines' hotel, rental car, credit card, and phone card partners. Some programs even allow you to earn miles on the interest you pay on your home mortgage.

- Join a frequent guest program, like Marriott Rewards, Hilton HHonors, or Hyatt Gold Passport. Hotel frequent stay programs are not nearly as popular as the frequent flier programs, but offer excellent benefits. According to a study by *Frequent Flyer* magazine, top benefits of hotel program memberships, in descending order of importance, include room upgrades; better choice of rooms; other special amenities (free breakfast, newspapers, calls, etc.); no-fee membership; and priority reservations or guaranteed room. Most hotel programs operate on number of stays versus number of nights. The best hotel programs offer merchandise rewards as well as free travel. Like the airline programs, elite levels in hotel programs (for as few as 15 stays per year) are worth aiming for, too.
- Most major hotel chains allow you to earn airline miles for hotel stays—not necessarily in conjunction with flights. With these programs, travelers must choose whether they want to earn airline miles *or* hotel program points, not both. Hilton and Westin are the only exceptions, allowing "double-dipping," or the opportunity to earn both hotel points and airline miles.

124—CHARGE YOUR WAY TO THE TOP

Use that affinity charge card to pay for everything! Here are some charge ideas to build up your card balance in order to earn more miles.

- Children's college tuition
- Airport parking
- Phone and utility bills
- Postage
- Car payments
- Groceries
- Charities
- Medical bills
- Prescription medicines

125—BEWARE OF EXPIRING MILES

Don't forget that millions of airline miles vaporize at the end of each year. Miles earned on United, American, America West, and Northwest expire after three years. However, miles earned before the mileage expiration policies went into effect (in 1988) do not expire. Currently Alaska, US Airways, Continental, and TWA have no expiration dates on their miles. Miles on Delta and Midwest Express expire only if you don't fly the carrier at least once every three years.

- If you're a mileage hoarder and have the majority of your miles in an expiring plan, go ahead and redeem as often as you can: use your miles for upgrades, for bringing along a spouse, or for merchandise.

- If you are sitting on a bank of miles that are about to expire, remember that you really have one year from the expiration date to take your free trip. This means you can go ahead and redeem your miles for a free trip certificate in December (even if you don't know where you want to go). Just don't convert the certificate into a free trip until you decide when and where you want to go. And if you want to really extend your expiration date, convert the certificate into a ticket for a trip. Once you have the ticket, you can cancel or change it for up to a year from the date of issue—but you'll have to pay the airline's ticket change fee (usually $50 to $75).
- Instead of letting those miles go poof, consider giving them to a good cause. Many airlines have formal programs where members can donate miles to specific charities—most of them related to reuniting families or providing once-in-a-lifetime trips for terminally ill children. Frequent fliers should contact their program service center for details.

126—WATCH THOSE TAXES Despite the introduction of a bill in 1996 to remove even the slightest notion that the IRS will *ever* tax frequent flier miles, the issue remains a gray area. Congress has not moved on the legislation, and the IRS tax code still hints at a desire to consider the freebies earned on business trips as a taxable employee benefit.

Now the IRS is going after miles on another front. Since late 1997, third-party purchasers of miles, like long-distance carriers, hotels, car rental companies, or banks, have been paying a 7.5 percent tax on the miles they buy from airlines and give to customers as incentives. Long-term effect: Instead of offering miles from 5 or 10 airlines to their customers, they could offer miles from just 1 or 2, thus saving taxes. That'll make earning miles in your favorite programs a little tougher.

Confessions of a Frequent Traveler: Los Angeles

Business travel does not have to be a bore. With a little creativity, planning, and some personal funds, even a mundane trip can be exciting. You've probably heard about how business travelers are adding minivacations to the front and back ends of their trips. But every now and then, I think it's a good idea to take a vacation *within* a business trip.

Here's what I mean. Recently I went to Los Angeles for a three-day meeting, and instead of going the "beige" route, I decided to splurge. My client offered what they would normally pay for a trip to Los Angeles—coach airfare, $150 a day for hotel, $35 a day for a car, $50 a day for meals and incidentals—but I upgraded the trip with my personal funds and frequent flier miles.

As long as I was in a place in the business of creating and promoting dreams, I thought I might as well live out a fantasy of being a movie magnate or entertainment type and let the business side of the trip subsidize the vacation side. Here's how you can do it too.

Airline

If you are flying nonstop from most major cities, know that first-class seats on most major-carrier nonstops to Los Angeles International (LAX) regularly sell out to paying passengers. If you are planning to use your miles to upgrade, you need to plan far in advance.

To get your trip started on an elite level, buy a full-coach ticket and use your frequent flier one-class-upgrade coupons. (Some airlines with one-stop service to LAX will upgrade passengers paying full-coach fares.)

Car

You must rent a car in Los Angeles—there's no way around it. But if you really want an LA experience, get a convertible. The latest, coolest car that hip business travelers are using to cruise LA's freeways? The Chrysler Sebring. (Try Avis, Thrifty, National, or Budget—or get a Mustang from Hertz.) Cost: about $60 per day—expensive, but worth it if you pay half and your company pays half.

Hotels

Hip haunts aren't cheap on the west side of LA. Most in spots start at around $250 per night. Steep, yes, but if your company is paying most or part of the tab, your contribution shouldn't be over $100.

New-World Hotel

The latest westside hotel for powerful young trendsetters is Shutters on the Beach in Santa Monica. The clubby lobby and restaurants are *the* place to see and be seen. (Don't forget your sunglasses.) Power brokers and writers are perched poolside with cellular phones and laptops beeping and buzzing. Rooms are equipped with two-line phones, voice mail, and 24-hour room service, and most have a view of the beach. For relaxation, rent a bike for a ride down to Venice Beach or enjoy a spa treatment. Other westside hotel ideas: the Mondrian or Beverly Prescott.

Old-World Hotel

For old-world charm, try the Bel Air—the genteel, old-money side of LA snuggled in a lush canyon just off Sunset Boulevard. Here you'll find 12 acres of rarefied opulence—gardens and private patios, with stars, starlets, moguls, and their handlers everywhere. (Marilyn Monroe's favorite bungalow has been revamped as the hotel's health club.) Despite its prices (starting at about $300 a night) the hotel enjoys the highest occupancy rate in Los Angeles (84 percent).

Dining

If the price of moguldom at a hot Hollywood hotel is too much for your budget, at least try the hotel restaurants. Weekday power breakfasts or weekend brunches are packed with the in crowd sporting their Gucci, Pucci, and Fiorucci—but this is California, so a jacket and tie are rarely required. If you want a colleague or client to snap to attention, invite her to breakfast at the Bel Air—a business tradition unmatched by any other restaurant in town.

Tasteful Tidbits

- *Bring sunglasses:* the hottest brands include Matsuda, Oliver Peoples,

Takumi, or Revo. (They'll make you look at home in your convertible.) Also, bring along your cell phone if you have one. It can be a savior when you're stuck in LA traffic.

- *Tipping:* Always have a pocketful of small bills for valet parkers (everywhere), bellhops, or other service providers.
- *Before you go:* For the latest Tinseltown goings-on, pick up a copy of *Buzz Magazine* from your local bookstore.
- *Free Time:* See the new Museum of Television and Radio in Beverly Hills.

CHAPTER 10

International Travel

Working or traveling overseas on business used to be the domain of "career expatriates"—you know, the James Bond international affairs types, probably not the best managers in the home office, but too smart or well connected to let go. These were the ones sent overseas. Now U.S. companies, saddled with saturated markets at home, are taking their international markets much more seriously. Faced with stiff competition from internationally savvy and powerful foreign companies, U.S. companies are sending their smartest, brightest, and even youngest employees on overseas assignments.

With the exception of the Japanese, U.S. citizens are about the only population that refers to travel outside our borders as "going overseas." Amazingly, only about 10 percent of U.S. residents own valid passports. Americans grow up without the easy cultural exchanges and experiences that those dwelling in most world regions can experience over a weekend or in an easy commute. The result is that we seldom go overseas prepared to understand, accept, or accommodate the workplace of a host country. Many learn the hard way that the American way is *not* the only way. Other nationalities are more accustomed to recognizing and accommodating the "ugly American" than we are of returning the favor.

An overseas assignment no longer means months or years abroad. With a shrinking world, it is now common for some managers to dart off to the other side of the world for a short period of time. Indeed, there is a small but growing number of business travelers who ply the north Atlantic weekly and consider it a commute.

For international travel to truly be a feather in the cap of a rising star, the trip must be successful. This chapter covers the basics, but in international travel, *specifics* are important. Before you embark on any trip abroad, read up on the minutiae. There are many good guidebooks, but don't discount a good novel that takes place in the country you are going to, a recent newspaper from the country, or a detailed magazine article. Even a long conversation with a recent returnee or citizen of the country to which you are traveling is an excellent idea. *Bon voyage!*

127—GET YOUR PASSPORT IN ORDER

- In 1998, new passports, good for 10 years, cost $60. Renewals are $40. For up-to-date information, ask your travel agent or call the

State Department's information line at 202-647-0518. You can also access information and applications online at www.travel.state.gov/passport_services.html or receive automated assistance from the National Passport Information Center (900-225-5674, 35 cents a minute). If you are applying for a passport for the first time, you must fill out your application and pay your fee at a passport agency or post office. Bring proof of U.S. citizenship (a certified copy of a birth certificate or a certificate of naturalization or citizenship); two recent, identical 2" x 2" front-view photographs with a light background (many post offices will now take your picture on-site), and proof of identity (a valid driver's license is sufficient).

- To renew your passport, fill out a renewal form, which you can get on-line or from most post offices or travel agencies. Send it to the passport agency address on the form with your old passport, two new 2" x 2" front-view photos, and a $40 check. Your new passport will be mailed to you. (*Note:* If you are sentimentally attached to your old passport, ask that it be invalidated and returned to you as well.)
- Passport offices are busiest from March through June. If you apply for your passport during this time, allow several weeks for delivery to avoid unnecessary delays. For an additional $35 fee, expe-

dited passport service ensures that you will receive your passport within two weeks. When applying in person for expedited service at a passport agency, you must present proof of necessity (usually plane tickets or an itinerary from the airline) along with the proof of citizenship and identification and the two photographs. Or you can apply at a court or post office and have your application sent to the nearest agency through the overnight delivery service of your choice. Make sure to include a self-addressed, prepaid envelope for the return of your passport.

- Alternately, your travel agent should be able to connect you with services that can help speed up the sometimes lengthy application process. For $50 to $200, these services walk your application through the issuing offices in one to five days. All you have to do is express-mail your completed application and photographs to them.

128—A VISA IS NOT A PASSPORT

- Know the difference between a *passport* and a *visa.* When the U.S. government gives you a passport, it is providing only a document that permits you to leave the country. A visa is an official authorization from another country, stamped inside your passport, that gives you permission to travel within that country for a specified purpose and a limited time. It is a good idea to contact the country's embassy or consulate closest to you for the most up-to-date information on visa requirements. Visa requirements are sometimes politically charged and can change with the change of government.

- In some countries, your contracts may be null and void if you signed them while traveling on the wrong type of visa (i.e., you are traveling on business, but hold a tourist visa). You could even run into problems expensing your trip with the IRS.

129—PREPARE FOR THE DIGITAL PASSPORT

As border crossers have done for years, business travelers treat their passports' immigration stamps like medals of honor. However, it looks like technology will soon eliminate that tradition—at least in the United States. Over the past few years, the U.S. Immigration and Naturalization Service (INS) has conducted a successful test of a new concept called INSPASS with frequent international travelers. Rather than using a passport, travelers are issued a special card that holds a digitized image of their handprint.

Upon arrival back in the United States, these travelers simply proceed to the nearest INSPASS kiosk, insert their card into the machine, place their hand on a reader, obtain approval, and go along their merry way—leaving less lucky travelers in their dust. As of the end of 1997, all three New York City airports and Toronto's Pearson International Airport were the only airports to have these systems installed. However, INSPASS should soon expand to Miami, Los Angeles, Honolulu, Houston, San Francisco, Chicago, Montreal, and Vancouver. Travelers from the United States, Canada, Bermuda, and 25 other countries are already eligible to enroll in INSPASS.

To obtain an INSPASS application form, write to USINS, INSPASS, P.O. Box 300766, JFK Airport Station, Jamaica, NY 11430, or simply download an application at www.usdoj.gov/ins/forms. After filling out the form, applicants must then go an enrollment center, located at most airports where INSPASS is accepted. Here a digital photograph is taken, as well as fingerprints and an image of the individual's hand geometry. If your application is approved, you will be issued a card on the spot.

130—PLAN AHEAD

- Before leaving, empty your wallet on to a photocopier and copy your credit cards, driver's license, and other essential documents. Also, copy your plane ticket, your passport, and your visa. Store these documents separately. If you ever lose your wallet or plane ticket, you will be eternally grateful for heeding this advice.
- For Internet-active business travelers, the Consular Affairs Web page provides up-to-the-minute information on security alerts, passports, visas, medical requirements, and other international travel matters. Log on to the site at www.state.gov to receive many helpful tips and services.

- If you're not connected to the Web, you can call the State Department's Citizen's Emergency Center, 202-647-5225, for a full menu of 24-hour-a-day recordings of all current travel advisories accessed by pushing the buttons on your phone.
- Keep the street address and telephone number of the U.S. embassy or consulate in the city where you are going in your wallet, separate from your passport.
- Know the emergency assistance numbers provided by your credit card company or travel agency. These numbers can be called collect for help on finding emergency medical or legal help overseas. Check with your insurance company to determine the limits of their coverage overseas. This goes for health, life, and car insurance.
- The British Airports Authority now provides airlines with fast-track passes that enable business and first-class passengers to bypass the sometimes enormous lines that form at customs and immigration upon entering the UK. (Coach passengers with elite-level frequent flier status should ask for fast-track cards at check-in in the United States.)

131—STAY HEALTHY

Becoming ill at home is an inconvenience. Becoming ill overseas can be a nightmare. The best advice is to prevent mishaps by planning ahead and taking some precautions.

- Get a checkup. Be sure that you are well enough to take a trip. Sometimes overlooked, but equally important: get a dental checkup.
- Check with the State Department (202-647-5225), the Centers for Disease Control (888-232-3228), or your local public health department to find out what vaccines or immunizations are needed or recommended for the countries in which you will be traveling. For the most part, you will not need any shots for trips to developed countries.
- Bring an ample supply of your prescription drugs. You cannot rely on the quality of drugs that you purchase overseas. To prevent any hassle at customs, it is important that your drugs are in the original, labeled containers with your name on them. Drugs that are legal in the United States could be illegal elsewhere.
- Consider medical evacuation insurance if you will be traveling to underdeveloped countries. Ask your travel agent how to purchase this.
- Keep up to date on all vaccinations (like tetanus) to avoid injections in foreign countries. If you must have a shot or other medical treatment, contact the local U.S. embassy or consulate for recommendations.

132—BE CAREFUL ABOUT WHAT YOU EAT AND DRINK . . .

Traveler's diarrhea is by far the most common travel-related illness. You are at greatest risk when traveling outside northern Europe, Canada, Australia, or the United States. Traveler's diarrhea is most often caused by eating foods contaminated with certain types of bacteria, but can also be caused by the stress or change of diet that come with any international trip. Here are some tips for avoiding diarrhea.

- It's a cliché, but when in suspect countries, don't drink the water. Don't eat the ice cubes. Don't brush your teeth with it. Don't even rinse your mouth out in the shower with it. Drink, brush, or rinse only with bottled, boiled, or treated water. Be sure that bottled water is opened in your presence.
- Avoid unpasteurized dairy products like milk, cream cheese, or pastries with cream or custard filling. Stay away from salad greens or raw fruit and vegetables.

133—AND ABOUT SEXUALLY TRANSMITTED DISEASES

Business travelers could be at greater risk of contracting AIDS and other sexually transmitted diseases than the general population. Why? Because of the loneliness of the road, casual sexual encounters and temptations to stray from monogamous relationships are more numerous. The following are some suggestions for decreasing the risk of contracting AIDS (and other sexually transmitted diseases) while on the road:

- Try to avoid sexual contact with casual acquaintances, and certainly avoid prostitutes. In some areas 90 percent of prostitutes are reportedly HIV-positive. If engaging in any sexual activity, use a condom *at all times.*
- Condoms purchased overseas aren't as reliable as those in the United States. Heat, light, and time will eventually render latex condoms useless. Many condoms now have expiration dates stamped on their packages. If you are sexually active, *always* have a fresh supply on hand. Protect your condoms and they will protect you.
- The traditional "booze, broads, and bribes" culture of business travel has all but disappeared in the United States. But overseas the tradition persists, particularly in parts of Asia. And these days, that tradition could prove lethal. Don't risk your life for a deal.
- For long-term assignments, some countries require proof that you test negative for HIV before granting you a work visa. For a complete list of international AIDS testing requirements, contact the Bureau of Consular Affairs, 2201 C Street NW, Room 5807, Washington DC 20520, or call 202-647-1488.
- Hepatitis A is caused by poor or nonexistent water purification processes. It can be transmitted by food, water, or human contact. Pretrip vaccines are available for travelers headed to regions with questionable sanitation.

- Hepatitis B is far more epidemic than AIDS and is much more easily transmitted than HIV. Business travelers headed to underdeveloped countries for prolonged periods should consider a hepatitis B vaccine, unless they are already immune. Many people are immune but don't know it; the only way you can find out for sure is to get a blood test. The vaccine, a series of three shots over a 6-month period, costs about $100 and is covered by most health insurance plans.
- Avoid any skin-puncturing activity like ear piercing, tattooing, acupuncture, manicures, or dental work, especially when traveling in less developed countries.

134—KNOW WEATHER CONDITIONS AHEAD

Check international weather by tuning in to CNN or the Weather Channel or visiting www.weather.com or cnn.com/weather on-line. You can also check *USA Today* or call 900-WEATHER (900-932-8437), which gives worldwide forecasts for 90 cents per minute. Remember that the seasons are reversed in Southern Hemisphere cities like Buenos Aires or Sydney and that rainy or dry seasons are the rule in many equatorial cities. Pack accordingly.

135—CHOOSE THE PROPER FINANCIAL INSTRUMENTS

The abundance of cheap international airfares is helping to keep the cost of going overseas at an all-time low. But the cost of staying overseas can become a burden that many business travelers can't afford. A good way to start saving money up front is to analyze the changing financial instruments available for international travelers and choose the ones that suit you best. Some considerations:

- Automated teller machines (ATMs) are currently your best deal for exchanging money because they dispense local currency—drawing on your home bank account—and give you the wholesale exchange rate, a preferential rate usually reserved for transactions of $1 million or more. This rate can be from 5 to 10 percent better than the rate you get at hotels or currency exchanges. Expect similar or slightly higher per-transaction fees than you are charged for ATM withdrawals at home. *Tip:* Be sure to deposit enough money in your checking account before you leave. The Cirrus and Plus networks are not combined outside the United States. To find out where you can use your Cirrus card outside the United States, call 800-424-7787, log on to www.cirrus.com, or call your bank. For the Plus system, call your bank or access the Web site via www.visa.com. International ATMs usually accept only four-digit PIN code numbers.
- Traveler's checks in U.S. dollar denominations are losing popularity because of bad exchange rates and usurious bank fees. You'll avoid potentially long waits in line, high fees, and bad conversion

rates (especially in the UK) by buying your traveler's checks at home in the currency of the country to which you are headed.

- U.S. dollars are widely accepted, and in some countries, they are even favored above local currency. Always try to purchase enough local currency in the United States to pay your cab fare from your destination airport to your hotel, plus a little extra for tips. This way you can avoid the lines that inevitably form at airport currency exchanges. (A growing number of international airports now have several ATMs in the terminal, but lines form at these, too.) At airport exchange booths, it is usually only possible to get the official rate (plus official surcharges), which vary greatly from what you may get "on the street." Ruesch International, a foreign exchange company, sells a variety of international currencies over the phone and will send your currency via overnight mail. Call 800-424-2923. Compare its exchange rate with that of your local bank.
- Spend or convert your foreign coins into bills before returning to the United States. Banks and foreign exchanges accept foreign *bills* only. Many airlines and airports have designated bins where your excess coins can be deposited as gifts to various charities.
- Cash advances on credit cards are a good idea only if you pay off your balance

every month. You can use your Visa or MasterCard, plus your personal identification number, to withdraw cash from more banks in more countries than you can with only an ATM card. American Express provides another network. For locations, call 800-CASH-NOW (800-227-4669). It charges a 2 percent fee on these transactions. However, cardholders can avoid the fee by cashing personal checks for local currency at American Express offices in most major cities around the world.

- If you pay with a credit card, you avoid fees altogether and get a potentially better exchange rate. If the dollar strengthens between the time you make your purchase and the time it is processed, you'll come out ahead (it also works in reverse, though). Most establishments frequented by business travelers around the world accept all major credit cards. However, don't expect the vast credit card culture that we enjoy in the United States to be the norm outside major cities or tourist areas overseas.
- If your hotel or rental car company takes your credit card when you check in, it could be blocking charges—possibly thousands of dollars—potentially preventing you from using your card elsewhere. To avoid this predicament, use cards with no preset credit limits, like American Express or Diners Club. When it comes time to settle your bill, you can put it on a credit card. (*Note:* AmEx and

Diners Club cards will sometimes "max out" if blocked charges exceed your average spending ceiling. If you know that you'll be spending a higher amount than usual, it's a good idea to call ahead of time and let them know.)

- Expect to see more of the euro—the new all-Europe currency—that is scheduled to replace local currencies in at least 11 of the European Union's 15 member states by 2002.

136—KNOW YOUR HOTEL

- Travelers in the United States are spoiled by low rates resulting from overbuilt markets in some cities. Hotel rates for business-class accommodations overseas are typically three or four times what you would expect to pay for a similar hotel at home. With demand outstripping supply, especially in major world capitals, business-class hotel rooms sell out fast—even at a premium.
- Before leaving home, ask your travel agent to determine if your hotel has an early check-in policy for international arrivals. Most flights from the East Coast to Europe leave the United States in the evening and arrive very early in the morning. Flights from the West Coast to Asia arrive early in the morning as well. There is nothing worse than the jet-lagged, sleep-starved purgatory of sitting in a crowded hotel lobby waiting for maids to clean your room. (*Note:* Some airlines now offer "daytime" transoce-

anic flights that take off from the United States first thing in the morning and arrive at your destination just in time for bed. Be sure to inquire about these flights.)

- Use the concierge at international hotels. You won't find a better source of local information or assistance.

137—UNDERSTAND INTERNATIONAL DRIVING

- U.S. state-issued driver's licenses are valid in most countries. If you aren't sure, call the American Automobile Association, which can issue you an international driving permit.
- Inquire about the type of car you will be renting. Many foreign locations rent only cars with manual transmissions. Check with your insurance company or credit card company before you go to determine coverage. (See Chapter 6, "On the Road," for more tips on renting a car overseas.)
- If you have several meetings at various locations in a foreign city, ask the hotel concierge to arrange a driver for you for the day, a common practice in many foreign cities. Renting a car and trying to navigate a foreign city could be a lesson in futility.

138—EDUCATE YOURSELF

- Before leaving the United States, hit the Internet or go to your public library and brush up on the politics, economy, geography, and language of the country you will be visiting. The ugly American, although a dying breed, is still the brunt of many jokes in international circles owing to our supposed insularity and ignorance of the world beyond our borders. To find a good novel that takes place in the country or region you are headed for, go to the on-line bookstore at www.amazon.com and search for the name of the country.

- Be inquisitive about your host culture. It will flatter your hosts. You'll be surprised to see the eyes of your host light up when you can say a few words in his language, correctly pronounce his president's or prime minister's name, or knowledgeably discuss the geography or cuisine of his homeland.

139—USE AN INTERPRETER Since the majority of Americans are not multilingual, an interpreter is usually necessary in business negotiations. Your hotel concierge should be able to arrange such services. To avoid confusing or offending your foreign counterpart, keep these tips from The Executive Speaker, a consulting company based in Orlando, Florida, in mind when using an interpreter.

- Don't try to make jokes that are regional, slangy, or sarcastic.
- Maintain eye contact with your counterpart, not the interpreter.
- Don't say things you wouldn't want your counterpart to hear. Many non-English

speakers can understand English but lack the confidence to speak it.

- Speak slowly and keep negotiations as concise as possible.

140—UNDERSTAND INTERNATIONAL PROTOCOL

The smart international traveler will do some cultural research to prevent committing embarrassing gaffes abroad. Business travelers need to be especially alert for behavior that could not only offend a host, but doom a deal. Your local bookstore travel section is full of helpful how-to guides for travel abroad, but most are written with the vacation traveler in mind. To find ones that are useful to the business traveler requires a little digging.

One excellent source of country-specific information are *Culturgrams,* published by the David M. Kennedy Center for International Studies at Brigham Young University in Provo, Utah. The short, four-page briefings have the unique ability to go beyond the superficial demographics and reveal a nation's personality, lifestyle, and culture. Each individual briefing paper is written by a native of the selected nation or someone who has lived there for at least three years and is fluent in one of its major languages. Every *Culturgram* is revised and updated yearly. Order *Culturgrams* individually ($6 each, including shipping and handling) or by the set (prices vary) by calling 800-528-6279.

141—KNOW HOW TO TREAT VISITORS TO THE UNITED STATES

Observing the culture of the country you will be visiting is essential; however, it is just as important to make international business associates feel comfortable when they visit the United States. Imagine yourself in this situation: you have just arrived in the States and you know a minimal amount of English. How would you feel if you were barraged by people using slang, local vernacular, idioms, and euphemisms and generally speaking at a pace that you found unintelligible? Here are some tips from Roger Axtell, an international protocol authority and author of the *Do's and Taboos* series of international travel guides published by John Wiley & Sons (800-225-5945).

- There are many ways you can help the international travelers you meet. Simply speaking slowly and clearly is the first step. Remember to enunciate all of your words, and be conscious of not dropping "ings" or running words together.
- Saying "gonna" or "shoulda" might confuse the uninitiated. Transition words like "um," "well," or "like" can also be tricky. And always be careful not to speak loudly in an effort to help the person to better understand you.
- Speaking on a first-name basis in a business setting is a typically American

trait, but be wary when dealing with northern Europeans, whose good English might make you feel comfortable. For these guests, it may be proper to wait until you are invited to use first names.

- Greetings differ from country to country. Learning a few simple phrases like hello, goodbye, please, or thank you in your guest's language is a great way to make a friendly gesture.
- Eye contact and body language also play a major role in conversation. Be aware of nods and facial expressions: they often say more than spoken words. And remember to smile. No matter what language someone speaks, they will always understand a smile.

142—LAPTOP TIPS Before you haul your laptop across the globe, there are a few things you should know in order to keep it running while you travel.

- To maximize your laptop battery life, discharge the battery a few days beforehand by leaving it on all night or until it crashes. Then recharge it fully in time for your flight (about 12 hours). Do this more than once if you have the time.
- While most laptops can convert to a higher European voltage without a converter, the socket designs and shapes vary throughout the world, making it impossible to plug your phone or electric line into the wall. To avoid this

hassle, call Road Warrior at 714-418-1400, or log on at http://warrior.com. They will mail you the correct adapters, modem plugs, and connectors you'll need for the countries you will be visiting. They will also send you a modem saver, which is an electronic device you can plug into your phone socket to see if it's compatible with your PC card modem.

- To ensure that you will be able to check your e-mail while you are traveling, subscribe to a worldwide on-line service, such as America Online, or other services that provide Web-based e-mail (i.e., e-mail that can be accessed from any computer with Internet access).

143—KNOW THE COST OF LIVING

Worried about what traveling overseas will cost you? Depending on where in the world you're traveling, costs can fluctuate greatly. Take a bottle of aspirin, for example. You might think that the cost would remain pretty standard. Not so. While a 100-count bottle of aspirin costs only $2.49 in Mexico, you'll pay a whopping $22.91 in Tokyo for the same product. Or how about a six-pack of beer? To give you an idea about how costs can vary from country to country, here's how much a six-pack costs in 11 cities in late 1997 (*source:* Runzheimer International).

Hong Kong:	$6.50
London:	$5.79
Los Angeles:	$4.18

Madrid:	$2.97
Mexico City:	$2.75
Munich:	$4.49
Paris:	$4.57
Rio de Janeiro:	$5.05
Sydney:	$6.81
Tokyo:	$11.07
Toronto:	$5.47

144—WOMEN TAKE NOTE Outside the U.S. and Canada and some northern European countries, women traveling on business do not usually receive the same amount of respect as their male counterparts. Although female business travelers account for one of the fastest-growing segments of the travel industry, the problem persists. One possible advantage to businesswomen encountering a foreign society is that their associates may be a bit curious and more apt to pay attention—and they may test their competence.

An informal poll of female business travelers conducted by the Air Travel Card provides these tips.

- Research the customs of the country you are visiting before boarding the plane. Familiarity with local and regional attitudes about women in business will help define your approach and avoid potential problems or embarrassing situations.
- When you arrive, observe local businesswomen and adapt your practices accordingly. Do not lose your identity, but be sensitive to the woman's role.

- In some countries it may be helpful (or the law!) to travel with a male escort who can serve as a buffer between the two societies. In some instances, having a man introduce you can immediately establish credibility in a business situation.
- Carry plenty of business cards with your business information printed on the reverse side in the official language of your host country. Your business card makes a professional impression, establishes credibility, and assists in introductions when conversing in a foreign language.
- Maintain your sense of humor! Often, problems on the road are a result of cultural differences and not sex discrimination. Try to defuse these incidents by keeping them in the proper context, then add them to your repertoire of international travel anecdotes.

145—PLAY IT SAFE IN UNFAMILIAR TERRITORY

- *Don't bring sensitive things to sensitive areas.* For example, don't try to bring a bottle of booze or a *Playboy/girl* magazine to an Islamic country. This is part of learning about the country before you go.
- *Beware of people causing distractions.* Scams used by pickpockets, thieves, and assorted ne'er-do-wells: an offer to brush lint off your suit; accidentally spewing catsup, mustard, or other condiment on your clothing; little old lady drops her

suitcase and you help her. Before you know it, you've been had. Also, crafty pickpockets will stand next to the signs that say Beware of Pickpockets just to watch where people feel to see if their wallet is still there. Then they know exactly where to "pick."

- *During times of heightened international tension, avoid public areas and keep a low profile.* Americans have a reputation for standing out. Try to blend in. Likely targets of terrorist activities are bus, train, and subway stations and government plazas. Many times disturbances will happen around public or religious holidays and controversial anniversary dates.

Confessions of a Frequent Traveler: Mexico City

Recently I traveled to Mexico City on business. It had been over three years since my last trip and I noticed a lot of changes, but I also noticed a lot of persistent problems that can make a business trip to this megacity live up to its reputation as a megahassle.

First, let's look at flying there. Mexico City's airport has always been and, I am afraid, still is chaotic on both arrival *and* departure, so always plan on delays.

After landing, I exited the jetway to a sea of arriving passengers and little indication (from signs or human beings) as to where to find customs, immigration, or the baggage claim. I finally found the crowded, noisy, and relatively long immigration lines: the Vienna Boys Choir had just arrived from Austria, causing even more playful confusion.

This was the first time I had to pause and use my travel-in-the-Third-World mantra: "This is *not* home, it's Mexico. It's *not* worse, just different!"

Once I made it past a grizzled but friendly immigration officer, I headed to customs. I got all the way to the exit, but was stopped there and asked for my special customs "form." Without it, I was told to go back to the entry, find the booth with the forms, find a pencil, fill it out (on my knee) and return.

Once I passed through that gauntlet (again), I was greeted by a sea of eager families waiting for loved ones to arrive. I fake-smiled and plowed my way through the crowd, bought a taxi trip ticket at the authorized booth (about $10), and headed into town.

The business-class hotel scene in Mexico City has gone through a true metamorphosis. Only a few years ago, most major U.S. or international chains existed only in the coastal resort cities. Now they are all over central Mexico City.

In 1995, the Four Seasons opened a new hotel in the Zona Rosa area, which used to be an upscale tourist district but is now quite seedy. Marriott opened two new properties in Mexico City in 1997: an on-airport standard Marriott and a J. W. Marriott in the central Polanco district across from Chapultepec Park, which is where I stayed.

Although pricey ($200), the hotel was a sea of calm in the midst of this bustling urban sprawl. Like many hotels in Mexico City, the lobby was large and ornate. (Interestingly, upscale Mexicans congregate in hotel lobbies on weekends at around 8 P.M., then head out to eat at around 10.)

I like nothing better than a brand-new hotel room, so I was in hog heaven here. As you would expect from a Marriott, once inside my hotel room, I could have been in any Marriott in the world. (But as a J. W. Marriott, this one was noticeably plush.)

The phone worked exactly as it does in U.S. hotels. It even included voice mail. I could connect my laptop to the Internet to send my column to the paper. CNN (regular, not international) buzzed in the background. Room service promptly delivered watery American-style coffee. Plus, I even earned my Marriott Reward points for the stay!

Getting back to the phone, I was lulled into a false sense of security. Because it was so easy to dial out using my phone card, I thought it would not cost much. But when I got my MCI bill, I saw that I had paid $40 for a 21-minute call to New York!

Doing business in Mexico is not as easy as it may be in many parts of the world. But just remember my mantra. It's a developing country. It's not worse, it's just different!

CHAPTER 11

Eating Well

Eating well can be one of the great joys of an otherwise monotonous trip, so always make an effort to get out and enjoy a good meal. It may be the closest thing to a cultural experience you'll have on your trips to the less exciting business travel destinations on your itinerary.

The United States has become a world-class diner's market. Indeed, the case can be made that the United States now holds the Dining Capital of the World title, not only in quality but in value and sheer variety of international and regional cuisine.

The reasons for this welcome development merit examination by business travelers, many of whom could qualify among the world's top unsung, but well-fed, restaurant critics. These are some of the factors that continue to drive U.S. culinary eminence.

- Widespread travel across the United States that has led to a greater focus on regional, homegrown foods and styles of eating
- Broad availability of fresh produce, meat, and other ingredients
- Superstar status of American chefs and acceptance of cooking arts as a valid career path
- Several decades of demographic and lifestyle changes that have created a generation accustomed to eating take-out and restaurant fare
- New waves of immigrant cultures bringing diverse and inexpensive strains of ethnic cooking from Asia, South America, the Caribbean, and Africa

Meals represent 13 percent of corporate travel budgets—the third largest category of spending after airfare and lodging, and even more than car rental, says consulting firm Runzheimer International. Overall, business travelers spend an average of $39 per day on meals.

146—FIND THE RIGHT MEAL

Perhaps the most up-to-date and authoritative voices in American cuisine belong to Nina and Tim Zagat, publishers of the well-known *Zagat Surveys.* Annually, they publish two national dining guides: *America's Top Restaurants* and *America's Best-Value Restaurants.* With input from nearly 30,000 frequent diners across the country, the two pocket-sized, easily packed books chart a unique, consumer-wise portrait of the food scene in 29 U.S. cities. If you are on a long-term assignment in one city or travel to one city frequently, you may opt for the more detailed individual *Zagat Surveys* covering 40 U.S. metropolitan areas. They are available in most major bookstores for $9.95 to $11.95. The national editions cost $12.95. (Call Zagat at 800-333-3421.)

Can't decide between bagels, Burmese, Thai, or tandoori and don't have a good hotel concierge to ask for advice? Now there are many sites online that you can browse to find the restaurant of your choice in many cities around the world. A few good ones:

- For a watered-down, on-line version of *Zagat Surveys,* log on at www.pathfinder.com/cgi-bin/zagat/homepage and scan by city, type of cuisine, and price range to find the restaurant that best suits your taste.
- Fodor's Travel Planner at www.fodors.com is an easy way to access restaurant information for the city in which you will be staying. Simply click on the city of your choice, then fill out a simple table that asks for the type of cuisine, location, and price range that interests you, and a whole list of restaurants sure to please your palate will appear. Similar information can be found at www.restaurantrow.com.
- If you plan to be on the road a lot, check out www.eathere.com before you leave home. This site offers information on a wide range of delicious roadside eateries, from burger joints to pizzerias to diners and coffee shops to truck stops. The list goes on and on.

- A savvy cabbie or good hotel concierge is always a good source.

147—PREPARE FOR EMERGENCIES Harried business travelers who juggle meetings with flight schedules and leave little time for healthy eating may find that all their haste may be making more "waist." Here are a few general tips to keep you eating right.

- Don't skip breakfast. A healthy breakfast helps boost your energy and control your appetite throughout the day. Eat a balanced meal such as muffins, cereal with milk, and juice.
- Avoid those cheap but deadly breakfast buffets heaped high with fried eggs, bacon, and hash browns. A breakfast like that will more likely slow you down than pick you up. A few chunks of pale, unripe cantaloupe is typically the healthiest offering you'll find on one of these groaning boards.
- Be choosy about restaurants. If you are not out to impress a client, family-style restaurants or cafeterias usually offer nutritional items like salads, steamed vegetables, and baked or grilled meats. There is usually a good, inexpensive, and interesting vegetarian restaurant near most college campuses.
- Check menus before you sit down. Steer clear of fatty foods like meats with gravy, cream sauces, fried foods, and heavy desserts. Airport restaurants, fast-food

establishments, and fern bars serve primarily high-fat, high-cholesterol fare.

- If you are picking up the tab, take the lead when ordering. If you decide to get the healthy choice, it's likely that everyone else at the table may tone down their appetite.
- Don't fall into the unhealthy trap of thinking you should order "the biggest" or "the most expensive" at restaurants simply because you're on an expense account or someone else is picking up the tab. Also, remember that you do *not* have to clean your plate.
- Pack some raisins, dried apricots, an apple, an orange, or a bagel in your briefcase or carry-on bag. This way you'll be less tempted by the high-fat, high-salt, high-preservative fare from airplane galleys or vending machines.
- When opening a sealed container on airplanes (like cream, salad dressing, or juice), be sure it is pointed *away* from that new suit you're wearing!
- Drink less. Business travelers tend to drink more on the road than at home. Alcohol is high in calories, magnifies the effects of jet lag, and generally slows you down. Try to drink more water and natural fruit juices instead, which will help energize you and keep you at peak performance levels.
- Avoid hotel minibars, usually crammed full of high-priced, high-sodium, artifi-

cially preserved snacks. Instead, visit a nearby market and buy some fresh fruit to snack on during your stay. If you do break down and drink one of those $3 cans of soda pop or $2 candy bars, replace it with the same store-bought item to save money.

- A growing number of hotels now stock minibars with helpful, inexpensive necessities, like mineral water, crackers and cheese, milk and cookies, pretzels and fruit juice—all at less than premium prices.
- And now, even nonfood items are making their way into the minibar, almost transforming them into personal in-room convenience stores. Depending on the hotel, you can now find disposable cameras, disposable razors, suntan lotion, condoms, Band-aids, "hangover kits," and playing cards.
- For longer stays, choose a hotel that offers kitchen facilities. With the option of preparing your own meals, you have more control over what you eat.
- Order your airline meals in advance. Most major carriers offer low-fat, low-cholesterol, or other special meals (See Chapter 5, "On the Plane"). Like the airlines, many hotel banquet facilities now accommodate requests for vegetarian, low-sodium, low-fat, or other meals. Inquire with the staff or meeting planner in charge of the meal at least 24 hours ahead of time.

- Choose restaurants with healthful alternatives to rich foods and sauces. Ethnic foods like Chinese, Thai, and Italian can offer good taste with relatively little saturated fat and cholesterol.

148—JOIN A DINING PROGRAM

Most major airline frequent flier programs now offer dining programs. These award a certain number of miles (from 3 to 10) per dollar spent at a few thousand restaurants in the United States. If you eat out a lot, whether in your hometown or when you're on the road, these programs are worth a look.

By now you've probably heard of discount dining cards administered by companies like CUC International, Dining à la Card, or Transmedia. Typically, these offer members a 20 percent discount at participating restaurants that are listed in a program directory. And now that these cards have teamed up with airlines, you can earn miles instead of getting the discount or rebate.

- American, Continental, TWA, and United dining programs are run by Dining à la Card. United and American offer the program for free. Continental and TWA offer a two-month free trial, then charge $49.95 per year. Not free, like some other programs, *but* you'll earn 10 miles per dollar spent on the entire tab, tip included. You'll only earn miles on your first monthly visit to any of the 6800 restaurants on the plan. Up to three credit cards can be linked to the program, eliminating the need to present your frequent flier card. What's best about the credit card-linked programs is that you can earn an additional mile per dollar spent using an airline-partnered card. For details, call American (800-439-2031), Continental (800-677-4848), TWA (800-804-7109), or United (800-555-5116).

- The Northwest and Delta dining programs are administered by CUC International. The programs are free to join and offer 3 miles per dollar spent on food, drinks, and tax, but not tip, at over 2500 restaurants. The best part of the deal? Currently, about half the participating restaurants offer a nice 500-mile bonus on your first visit. You show your frequent flier card when paying the bill. Miles appear on your statement within four to six weeks. Since this is a free program, it's worth the time it takes to sign up. Call Northwest (800-289-6902) or Delta (800-346-3341).

The upside of these programs: they are a great new way to earn miles. The downside: some participating restaurants are not consistently popular or very "in" places. *Best advice:* Double-check your selection before heading out to eat. Ask a local to take a look at your guide and pick out a top spot.

149—AIRPORT MORSELS

Just a few years ago dining at the airport was like eating at a hospital or college dorm: you were lucky to find a few wedges of dried-out pizza or a wizened wiener. The only alternatives were the overpriced, full-service airport restaurants full of tired waitresses in white orthopedic shoes serving up plates of Salisbury steak and overcooked veggies. Yuck!

Airport food service has come a long way since airport authorities brought in brand-name establishments that serve up food the way we like it, or at least the way we are used to it. Check out these examples.

- *Atlanta-Hartsfield:* Wendy's, Chili's, Houlihan's, Burger King, TCBY, Au Bon Pain, Chick-fil-A, Domino's
- *Boston-Logan:* Legal Sea Foods, TCBY, Dunkin' Donuts, Burger King, Pizza Hut, Au Bon Pain, Cheers Bar, Samuel Adams Pub
- *Chicago-O'Hare:* Gold Coast Dogs, McDonald's, Pizzeria Uno, Starbucks, Peggy Sue's Diner
- *Dallas/Ft. Worth:* Freshens Yogurt, Burger King, TGI Friday's, Pizza Hut, McDonald's, Taco Bell, Au Bon Pain, Wendy's
- *Los Angeles International:* McDonald's, Wolfgang Puck's, Creative Croissants
- *Newark International:* Taco Bell, Pizza Hut, TCBY, Mrs. Fields, Au Bon Pain, McDonald's, Sbarro, Nathan's Famous Hot Dogs
- *Washington National:* Vie de France, Cheesecake Factory, Jerry's Subs and Pizza, Frank & Stein, McDonald's

150—MORE QUICK FIXES In response to passenger gripes about in-flight food cutbacks, many airports have set up portable carts that sell deli sandwiches, bottled water, juices, cookies, and snacks. These are great waystations if you are between short flights without meal service and haven't had a chance for a bite. On many of its German flights, Lufthansa serves a free buffet-style breakfast at the gate, offering a healthy board of yogurt, fresh fruit, breads, cereal, and coffee.

151—GO NATIVE With the influx of foreign business travelers, hoteliers and airlines are now expanding their offerings to help satisfy the cravings of their international guests. International food offerings provide an interesting option for travelers who want to make an otherwise mundane business trip into a bit of an adventure.

- Many Westin Hotels & Resorts now serve an authentic Japanese breakfast featuring pickled vegetables, rice, fish sausage, and roasted seaweed.
- *Bunderfliesch,* thin slices of air-dried beef, and *Birchermuesli,* a mixture of yogurt, nuts, grains, and dried fruit popular with Europeans, are available at Swissotels in the United States.
- Northwest and Delta provide Japan-bound business-class passengers with *makanouchi,* a chilled meal consisting of shrimp or sliced beef, rice, pickled vegetables, and miso soup served in a

black lacquered box. They are also available to passengers taking only the domestic leg (i.e., Atlanta to Los Angeles) of these international flights.

152—EATING OUT ALONE IS OKAY

One of the banes of the business travel experience is the trauma of having to eat out alone. Have you ever returned to your hotel after a long day's work and thought you would skip room service and just step down to the street for a bite at that corner bistro but could not bear the thought of sitting alone? It doesn't have to be that way. Here are some solutions.

- Find friends. Sit at sushi bars or captain's tables to find other lonely souls looking for dinner mates.
- Bring something to do. A book, magazine, or other light reading will ease your feelings of awkwardness or loneliness.
- Avoid high-priced, exclusive restaurants if you can. A fast and friendly establishment like TGI Friday's or Bennigan's isn't so bad, especially if you sit at a table in the bar area. A TV in the bar usually helps. You get your food fast and can get out of there fast.
- Eating alone in a hotel restaurant isn't as severe because it is more likely that several other people will be eating alone too. Staff at hotel restaurants are more accustomed to requests for a table for

one. If the hotel you are in doesn't have a restaurant, head to a nearby hotel with one.

- Get used to it. Veteran business travelers claim that after a while, they cross a threshold, and eating out alone doesn't really bother them anymore.
- Call your friends, or a friend of your friends. Invite them to go out with you.
- If all else fails, try room service. Remember that you don't always have to go by the measly room service menu usually offered. You can ask for almost anything you want.
- Cook in your room. With average guest stays of around 14 days, extended-stay hotels with kitchens or kitchenettes allow business travelers the luxury of an almost home-cooked meal. Some even provide grocery services.

153—FAMILIAR FOOD=FAMILIAR PRICES

For those who choose to eat fast food on their round-the-world journey, here's what they can expect to pay for a cheeseburger, soft drink, and french fries in 10 different cities in 1998 (*source:* Runzheimer International.)

Hong Kong	$2.81
London	$6.10
Los Angeles	$4.40
Madrid	$5.19
Mexico City	$4.00
Munich	$5.98

Paris	$6.25
Rio de Janeiro	$4.48
Sydney	$4.32
Tokyo	$6.32
Toronto	$4.02

Confessions of a Frequent Traveler: Sydney

In late 1997 I had an interesting "tables-turned" experience. I was invited to Sydney, Australia, home of the 2000 Summer Olympics, for a media tour. I remembered when the media started to trickle into Atlanta (my hometown) before the 1996 Summer Games. Now it was my turn. On the day I arrived, Sydney started its 1000-day countdown to the Olympics.

In the week that I was there, I experienced déjà vu almost every day. First, the Australians are jittery over an issue called "native title." Seems that the Aborigines, the indigenous peoples of Australia, are making native claims to land now owned by descendants of English settlers—and not getting very far. The controversy surrounding the issue reminds me of the shame and worry Georgians felt over flying the "stars and bars" Georgia state flag over the Olympics.

A rail link is being constructed between Sydney's Kingsford-Smith Airport and downtown to accommodate Olympic visitors. When a tunnel collapsed, almost killing two workers, a debate was immediately sparked over whether it is worth sacrificing human lives in order to host the Olympics. I remembered when a light tower collapsed during construction of our Olympic stadium, killing a worker.

"Official" Olympic merchandise is already dominating all the tourist shops. (Okay, I admit it. I bought a T-shirt.) There are classified ads in local newspapers soliciting home owners to rent their properties during the games. Every new hotel construction or revamp is scheduled to finish "in time for the Olympics."

Airlines

Qantas, stung by the fact the upstart national carrier Ansett Australian won the title of Official Carrier of the 2000 Games, is rolling out a world-class upgrade to welcome Olympic guests. Food (one of the best parts of any trip to Australia) reflects the fresh bounty available there. Flight attendants are trained in the art of fresh-food preparation on planes (less hot plate out of the oven, straight to the tray table. More slicing fresh fruit on board, baking bread and cookies).

New menus and focus on freshness are part of Qantas' teaming up with Sydney's trendy Rockpool Restaurant (great spot for a business lunch). Like California, Australia really has no true cuisine of its own, so food at top restaurants (and on Qantas) is always an eclectic mix of the freshest seafood, produce, and meat imaginable.

Flying some of the longest flights in the world (14 hours nonstop from LA to Sydney, for example), Qantas took a cue from partner British Airways and installed 6-foot-plus beds in first class and large, electronically controlled seats in business class.

Hotels

When I lived in Australia for the first time in 1987, there was only one truly world-class luxury hotel, the Regent, in Sydney. Now that Sydney is in the eye of the world (both *Condé Nast Traveler* and *Travel and Leisure* named it the world's top destination among readers in 1997), new business-class hotels have sprung up all over. Ritz Carlton has two properties in the city. Park Hyatt, ANA, Renaissance, and Inter-Continental have arrived on the scene to provide stiff competition to the Regent.

Named the Official Hotel of the 2000 Olympics, the Regent is scheduled for a $60 million makeover before the games. Right now, the Regent has the best location of any hotel in the city—smack between the financial district, the stock market, and an upscale nightlife-and-tourist mecca called The Rocks.

Transport

Unlike most U.S. taxi services, cabs in Sydney are fantastic, clean, and courteous. Drivers don't expect any more tip than rounding the fare up to the nearest dollar. Best of all, cabs are not allowed to be any more than six and a half years old. Airport to town: about $15.

With the coming of the Olympics, Sydney's extensive rail system will soon have a much-needed link to the airport. Another new rail link is expected to transport up to 36,000 passengers an hour to the Olympic Stadium, Village, and most venues (located on the site of an old dump in suburban Sydney) about a half-hour drive from downtown. In addition, downtown (the CBD, or central business district, in Sydney-speak) will be linked to the Olympic Village via high-speed ferry.

CHAPTER 12

Your Heart, Your Mind, and Your Body

While business travel is usually an incredible opportunity to grow professionally, it's easy to forget about nurturing other aspects of your life—like your family, your body, and your soul. The most successful business travelers pay attention to keeping their lives in balance.

Business travelers are taking more trips than ever, and with that additional workload comes an abundance of—you guessed it—stress. Seasoned road warriors who realize that "all work and no play" isn't necessarily the best way to conduct business (especially when "all work" leads to headaches, aching muscles, and burnout) are seeking solutions that don't take all the fun out of their busy business trips. Not surprisingly, almost two-thirds of 500 executives surveyed by Hyatt Hotels say that it's hard to stay on diets or eat nutritious food when they travel, and some 30 percent say they drink more often during road trips than they would if they were back home.

If you're a suffering nomad striving for balance, consider the following.

154—YOUR FAMILY

Feel riddled with guilt every time you see the sad eyes of your spouse or children peering out the window as you sling your suitcase in the car and speed off on another business trip? Both AT&T and MCI have come out with tips to help deal with the separation. (Not surprisingly, they lean toward using the phone!) AT&T asked 500 children ages 6 to 12 how they feel when their parents travel. Over half said they feel "very sad" about it, and 62 percent said they want the traveling parents to stay in touch more often. And don't bring home a T-shirt: While 39 percent of kids say that's what Mom or Pop usually brings home, only 7 percent say it's what they really want. Some other advice:

- Have a set time to call home each day—just before bedtime is good for young kids. Kids are very adept at the information superhighway. If you are traveling with a computer, communicate with them via e-mail or an on-line service. Have them fax you their report card or a paper they wrote in class.
- Videotape special occasions, send postcards, bring home gifts, save memorabilia, bring along pictures or children's drawings, and send flowers. Set up family Web pages and chat on-line. Hide

notes or gifts at home and call in your instructions on how to find them. Record yourself reading bedtime stories on video or audio tape to be played while you are away. Post a map and a calendar so children can see where you are and mark off the days until you return.

- Bring along a family member every now and then, if possible. Many conventions and hotels now provide child care. It's psychologically beneficial for family members to see what you do while traveling. It can ease their feelings of resentment and your feelings of guilt.

155—KEEP THE HOME FIRES BURNING

After a grueling week on the road, a business traveler looks forward to rest and relaxation at home. But the stay-at-home spouse, eager to make up for lost time, expects a lot of quality time from the traveling spouse. These differing expectations can wreak havoc on what should be "loving" homecomings. If you love your frequent flier balance as much as your significant other, here are some ways to keep the home fires burning.

- *Send flowers.* Most major airline frequent flier programs offer around 500 miles for FTD orders. Others offer a set amount of miles per dollar spent.
- *Make reservations.* Over the last year, most airlines have launched dining programs, offering from 3 to 10 miles for each dollar spent at restaurants in

almost every city. Present your frequent flier card when paying the tab, and get miles posted to your account automatically. (See Chapter 11, "Eating Well," for details.)

- *Phone home.* A call from 35,000 feet makes anyone feel special, and now you'll earn miles when using the seatback phone on some airlines. Also, most calling cards (and even some pay phones) allow callers to program a message to be delivered at any time. If you will be on an extended trip or otherwise out of touch, leave a short "I love/miss/can't-wait-to-see/am-thinking-of you" message for each day that you are away.
- *Bring him or her along.* If you are out on the road, instead of going home for the weekend, invite your special someone to join you. Call your hotel and ask for special weekend day rates. If you end up staying over a weekend, your air fare could be cut in half or more, so bringing along your mate might even save money—not to mention your relationship!

156—BE CONSIDERATE OF THE ONE AT HOME

Be considerate when asking to be picked up or dropped off at the airport. It takes a *lot* of time and energy to drive to the airport, fight traffic, kiss you goodbye, and drive home, especially during rush hour. Consider a cab or a car service, or drive yourself. Here are some other tips for getting along with a stay-at-home spouse.

- There is nothing worse than sitting in a crowded airport when you aren't even on a trip. If you are getting picked up at the airport, be sure to tell your spouse to call the airline ahead of time to determine if the plane will be arriving on schedule. As a simple courtesy, always provide your travel agent's or airline's 800/888 number.
- Let your spouse track your frequent flier programs for you. That way he can monitor the points and look forward to a time the points can be used on a joint trip.
- Beware of the "eat at home or eat out" debate. You eat out all week and want to eat at home on the weekends. Your spouse has probably eaten in all week and wants to go out on the weekend. *Solution:* Compromise. Set a schedule to eat in every Friday night and go out on Saturday night.

157—COPY THIS PAGE

Now, any relationship is a two-way street, so here are some things that a stay-at-home spouse can do to spruce up his or her mate's less-than-glam on-the-road existence.

- Call the hotel and have breakfast-in-bed delivered to your business traveler's room.
- Send your mate a love note via overnight mail, delivered to the hotel.

- Send flowers to the hotel. (Best to send notes and flowers to the hotel instead of the office to avoid potential embarrassment.)
- Prepay for a massage, facial, or spa treatment at the hotel if they offer it.
- Call the hotel and pay for an upgrade to a suite, or call your travel agent or airline and pay for an upgrade to first class.
- Leave a love note in her toilet kit, briefcase, or suitcase.

158—YOUR MIND

Stress, that feeling of being overwhelmed by the responsibilities and problems of everyday life, can have a serious negative impact on mental and physical health, not to mention productivity. Much research has been done on how life on the road affects frequent travelers and their families.

Atlanta therapist Deborah Butler offers these general issues to concentrate on when battling the stress of a life on the road.

- *Diet:* Don't go overboard when traveling. Take advantage of the new lighter-fare menus. Avoid the depressive effect of alcohol.
- *Exercise routine:* Try to stick to your at-home routine when you're on the road.
- *Meditation and journaling:* Make time to sit quietly and reflect on the day, or keep a daily journal of your thoughts and feelings.

- *Support group:* Find other frequent travelers to share your feelings with. Remember, you are not alone in your frustration.
- *Environmental control:* Bring along a picture of your spouse and put it on your bedside table, or bring along a small pillow. Try to impose your own environment on the ever-changing, on-the-road environment. Manage your environment instead of letting it manage you.

159—TAKE IT EASY

Here are some more tips on dealing with a life of business travel.

- Don't try to cram all your travel into one day. Sometimes it's worth the expense to arrive the night before and get a good night's sleep. Hilton offers Sleep Tight rooms at seven major U.S. hotels. Each room is equipped with special mattresses, sound machines, circadian light boxes—and milk and cookies in the minibar!
- Don't stress out about making "too many long-distance calls." Set up an answering machine at home and check your messages regularly. Return calls from afar. The telephone is your connection to your personal life, which needs to be nurtured, not ignored, even when you are away.
- In the current environment, it is inevitable that you will encounter delays.

Always come prepared with pleasant distractions like a book, a magazine, a new software game or program on your laptop, a new tape or CD for your Walkman, or a project that you are working on.

- Don't feel guilty about taking a break. Attend a local sporting event, see a movie, visit old friends, go to museums or libraries, or walk through interesting neighborhoods or markets. Try to restore a sense of adventure to your trip.

160—CHECK YOUR STATE OF MIND

The Hyatt Travel Futures Project survey of 700 business travelers found that some are less prone to stress than others. The most successful frequent travelers are flexible and easygoing and actually enjoy a certain amount of pressure. The survey found that some business travelers take their business trips too seriously. They tend to make the trips the focus of their lives, instead of accepting business travel as a part of their normal routine. Well-adjusted travelers are those who have learned to anticipate and handle uncertainties, have a good sense of humor, and are realistic about the business world and its limitations.

According to research by Residence Inns, women traveling on business enjoy leaving the responsibilities of keeping house at home. While on the road they are able to focus on themselves or on their work without domestic distractions. "The in-room experience can be more nourishing to a woman than a man," says project consultant Dr. Ron Jones.

161—STAY FIT The best way to reduce travel-related stress is to stay in peak condition. "Frequent travelers should shape up for the rigors of the road like athletes train for the rigors of competition," says Atlanta corporate fitness instructor Alice Stephens. Indeed, a strong, healthy body can handle stress better than a weak one. Here are some tips for staying fit in flight.

- Be aware of how you sit on the plane (or in your car). Good posture is essential when battling the stress associated with sitting in cramped quarters for hours. On long flights, try some in-seat movements (shoulder and head rolls, knee lifts, systematic tensing and relaxing of different muscle groups, especially your legs), and move around the airplane cabin as much as possible. This will prevent blood clots from forming in your legs—a life-threatening condition also known as *deep venous thrombosis.* Another way to avoid this problem is to take two aspirin, which thins your blood, before your flight.
- To prevent dehydration, drink one 8-ounce glass of water or juice for every hour you are in flight. Alcohol, caffeine, and some nasal decongestants can magnify dehydration. Contact lens wearers should carry extra saline solution—or better yet, wear glasses on the plane.
- In flight, breathe through your nose instead of your mouth. The nose is the body's first and best defense against

concentrations of airborne germs in the recirculated cabin air.

- For back support, place a small pillow in the seatback just above your pelvis. To prevent pressure on the sciatic nerve, men should move wallets from their back pocket. Suffer from swollen feet and ankles? Both men and women should consider wearing elastic or support hose on long flights. Another way to avoid "the bloat": avoid high-sodium snacks like pretzels and peanuts, as well as that salty bloody Mary.
- When you land, find a quiet smoke-free space for some deep-breathing exercises. This should help get your blood gases back to normal and reduce stress.
- Many airlines are spending millions of dollars to provide heart defibrillators on each plane and train flight attendants to use them. But the Air Transport Association says that in-flight medical emergencies are rare. Only 1 in every 5.8 million passengers experiences a problem. Based on information from 1996, when U.S. airlines carried 580 million passengers, the ATA says that there were 2,136 reported incidents of dizziness or fainting, 438 respiratory problems, 433 incidents of chest pain, 201 asthma attacks, 190 diabetic incidents, 141 heart attacks, 75 allergy attacks, and 49 headaches.

162—ASK A DOCTOR

Getting sick when you are away from home, or even worse, in a foreign country is no fun. One good way to find help if there's not a doctor in the house is Hotel Docs. You can reach them at 800-HOTEL-DR (800-468-3537). For $150 (covered by most medical insurance) one of their 2000 on-call physicians and specialists will come to your hotel.

If you've brought along your laptop, you can now log on for help. CyberDocs employs American board-certified emergency medical specialists who can answer questions on line, initiate treatment for minor illnesses, and even authorize delivery of some prescription medications. Cost in 1998: $50 per "virtual housecall," paid by credit card. See www.cyberdocs.com.

163—MAINTAINING YOUR EXERCISE REGIMEN

What with long flights, all-day meetings, and big sit-down meals, business travel is a big contributor to the "sedentary lifestyle" our doctors warn us against. Here's how to make the best of this situation.

- Remember, traveling itself takes a toll on your body. Don't work out any harder on the road than you do at home. Always remember to warm up and cool down slowly.
- Ask about your hotel exercise room, gym, or fitness center when you make your reservation. Some hotel fitness centers offer no more than a vacant room outfitted with a few weight machines

and treadmills. Others go out of their way to offer state-of-the-art facilities.

- At more luxurious hotels, you can request fitness equipment in your room. Other less luxurious in-room options to bring from home: jump ropes and aerobic dance or yoga tapes. An in-room exercise manual at Residence Inns (called *Inn Shape*) exhorts "phone book leg lifts, lower-abdominal bed crunches, and shoulder and tricep towel extensions," as part of the American Heart Association's recommendation of 30 to 60 minutes of exercise three to four times a week. (For a free guide, call 301-380-4536.)
- Does your health club at home have reciprocal agreements with others around the country? Find out before you leave home. (The venerable YMCA has one of the best reciprocal programs around—especially if you frequent major cities.) To locate facilities in your travel destination, check out *The Fitness Guide: Where to Work Out When You're on the Road* by Kyle Merker (Incline Press Publishing, 212-675-4378, retailing for $14.95). It includes information on hotel exercise facilities, health clubs, local gyms, and fitness classes in the 45 most popular U.S. destinations. On the Web, see the gym locator at www.globalfitness.com. Just enter the city and zip of your hotel and you get a list of clubs in the area.

- Indulge yourself with a massage, whirlpool, or sauna if your hotel offers them. These can reduce the physical tension of sitting for long periods in stuffy planes and airports.

164—ASK ABOUT SMOKING FLIGHTS AHEAD OF TIME

If you have grown accustomed to smoke-free flying on domestic routes, you may be startled to board international flights and find cigarette smoke once again curling from behind your seatback. While in-flight smoking has been snuffed out almost universally, there are pockets of resistance on some routes to Japan and South America. Always inquire about this when making your reservation.

165—DON'T LET JET LAG BE A DRAG

Jet lag can occur on transcontinental or transoceanic flights. Veteran transatlantic travelers usually agree that jet lag is more common after the flight to Europe (eastbound) than after the flight home. The same goes for transpacific flights: your westbound journey over there is easier than your eastbound journey home. As a general rule, it takes one day for your body to adjust to each time zone crossed. Here are some things that you can do to minimize the effects of jet lag.

- Flights from the United States typically arrive in Europe or Asia early in the morning. Don't plan on conducting too much important business the day you arrive. Instead, use that day to get your circadian rhythms in sync.

- The most popular jet lag remedy? *Denial!* Avoiding alcohol and regulating your diet and exposure to sunlight are a central theme in the many popular methods for dealing with jet lag. Alcohol consumption compounds your body's confusion and adds to dehydration. Some programs claim that different foods and caffeine, used accordingly, can help.
- Taking long walks outdoors or sitting near a large window sends light signals to your body. Some travelers sleep with room drapes open to let sunlight wake them up—and help reset their internal clocks.
- Aromatherapy is an increasingly popular treatment as scientists discover that certain scents can alter brainwave activity into rhythms that produce calmness or a sense of well being.
- There is new hope that melatonin, a hormone that helps regulate the sleep-wake cycle, can help eliminate jet lag. Because melatonin mimics seratonin, a hormone your body releases naturally as the sun goes down, a dose at bedtime at your new destination can help induce a good night's sleep and help reset the body's circadian rhythms to the new time zone. You can buy melatonin tablets at your local health food store for about $12 for a small bottle.

- Some people need the hard stuff. Seventy-nine percent of sleep experts surveyed by the Gallup Organization recommend short-acting prescription sleep medications to help their patients sleep on long night flights. Ambien, Halcion, and Valium are commonly prescribed. Business travelers should avoid over-the-counter sleep aids and "night-time" cold medicines as they tend to dry out nasal passages, and usually induce a hangover effect.

Appendix

Here are some sources for further information.

CHAPTER 1

Publications

- *Consumer Reports Travel Letter* ($39/year, tel: 800-234-1970)
- *InsideFlyer* ($36/year, tel: 800-767-8896)
- *Frequent Flyer* ($24/year, tel: 800-323-3537)
- *The Ticket* ($34/year, tel: 404-327-9696)
- *Best Fares* ($49.95/year, tel: 800-635-3033)
- *Business Travel News* ($95/year, tel: 800-447-0138)
- *Travel Weekly* ($29/year, tel: 800-360-0015)

Travel Sites On-Line

- Business travel booking: www.thetrip.com and www.biztravel.com
- General travel booking: www.travelocity.com, www.expedia.com, www.itn.com, www.americanexpress.com, or www.previewtravel.com
- Travel news: www.usatoday.com, www.cnn.com, www.cnnfn.com, or www.msnbc.com

- Airport and airline sites: www.airlines-online.com

Web sites for specific airlines:

Alaska	www.alaska-air.com
American	www.aa.com
America West	www.americawest.com
Continental	www.flycontinental.com
Delta	www.delta-air.com
Northwest	www.nwa.com
Southwest	www.iflyswa.com
TWA	www.twa.com
United	www.ual.com
US Air	www.usairways.com

Pet Sitters

National Association of Professional Pet Sitters: 800-296-PETS or www.petsitters.org

CHAPTER 3

Car Services in New York

The Yellow Pages lists car services in many cities. Here are three reliable ones in New York.

Absolute: 800-ABSOLUT

Big Apple: 800-692-3462

Carey Limousine: 212-599-1122

Tel Aviv: 212-777-7777

Some other useful organizations:

- Super Shuttle: 800-258-3826, www.supershuttle.com

- Salk International's *Airport Transit Guide,* PO Box 1388, Sunset Beach, CA 90742; tel: 800-962-4943; Web site: www.io.com/salk
- QuickAid automated service system, Los Angeles International Airport: 310-646-5252

CHAPTER 4

- Rules of the Air: www.rulesoftheair.com
- *Official Airline Guide:* 800-323-3537
- Weather Channel: 900-WEATHER, www.weather.com
- Complaints: U.S. Department of Transportation, C75, Room 4107, Washington, DC, 20590; tel: 202-366-2220
- Online airline and airport addresses: www.airlines-online.com

CHAPTER 5

Here's more help for the fearful traveler:

Magellan's Travel Catalogue: 800-962-4943

Pegasus Fear of Flying Foundation, 200 Eganfuskee St., Jupiter, FL 33477; tel: 800-FEAR-NOT

American Airlines Fearless Flyers: 817-424-5108

CHAPTER 6

Rental Car Services

- Hertz: www.hertz.com

- Avis: www.avis.com
- Alamo: www.goalamo.com

Mobile Office Environments: 800-373-9635

CHAPTER 7

Some useful sites:

- Hotel Reservations Network: 800-964-6835, www.180096hotel.com
- Quikbook: 800-789-9887
- New York Convention and Visitors Bureau: 800-846-ROOM
- Hotel Reservations

  Courtyard by Marriott: 800-321-2211, www.courtyard.com

  Hampton Inns: 800-426-7866, www.hampton-inn.com

  La Quinta Inns: 800-687-6667, www.laquinta.com

  Wingate Inns: 800-228-1000, www.wingateinns.com

  Budgetel: 800-428-3438, www.budgetel.com

  Days Inn Business Place: 800-329-7466, www.daysinn.com

  Fairfield Inn by Marriott: 800-228-2800, www.fairfieldinn.com

  Holiday Inn Express: 800-465-4329, www.holiday-inn.com

  Microtel: 888-771-7171, www.microtelinn.com

Red Roof: 800-843-7663, www.redroof.com

Sleep Inn: 800-627-5337, www.sleepinn.com

CHAPTER 9

Check out these for frequent travelers.

- Frequent Flyer Services: 719-574-6947
- *Frequent Flyer Guidebook:* 800-333-5937, www.insideflyer.com

CHAPTER 10

Passport Information

- State Department: 202-647-0518, travel.state.gov/passport_services.html
- National Passport Information System: 900-225-5674
- INSPASS: U.S. Immigration and Naturalization Service (INSPASS), PO Box 300766, JFK Airport Station, Jamaica, NY 11430; www.usdoj.gov/ins/forms

Health and Disease Information

- State Department: 202-647-5225
- Centers for Disease Control (CDC): 888-232-3228

Other Useful Sites for Travel Abroad

- Bureau of Consular Affairs: 2201 C Street NW, Room 5807, Washington, DC 20520; tel: 202-647-1488

- Cirrus: 800-424-7787, www.cirrus.com
- Plus: www.visa.com
- Ruesch International: 800-424-2923
- American Express ATMs: 800-CASH-NOW
- Culturgrams: 800-528-6279
- Road Warriors: 714-418-1400

CHAPTER 11

Where to Eat

- Zagat: 800-333-3421, www.pathfinder.com/cgi-bin/zagat/homepage
- Fodor's Travel Planner: www.fodors.com
- Eat Here: www.eathere.com
- Airline frequent flier dining programs
  Continental: 800-677-4848
  TWA: 800-804-7109
  United: 800-555-5116
  Northwest: 800-289-6902
  American: 800-267-2606
  Delta Airlines: 800-346-3341

CHAPTER 12

Staying Well

- Hotel Doctors: www.hoteldocs.com
- Virtual Doctors: www.CyberDocs.com
- Incline Press Publishing: 212-675-4378
- Fitness: www.globalfitness.com

INDEX

Absolute Car Service, 40
Advance purchase airfares, 10–12
Aerophobia, 87–89
Affiliations, for best rates, 105, 118
Affinity charge cards, 166
Agents, travel, 9–10
AIDS, 181–183
Air Canada, 75, 81
Air France, 46, 81
Air pressure, and ears, 84–85
Air Transport Association, 226
Air Travel Consumer Report, 18, 57
Air Travel Card, 194
Airfares:
- creative strategies, 13–14
- discount, 7–8, 11–12
- types, 10–11

Airline clubs, 68
Airline reservations, 10–11, 22–23
Airline tickets, 8–9, 69
Airlines, 169–170
- addresses/telephone numbers, 65
- booking, 7
- bumping, 59–61
- cabin pressure, 84–85
- carry-on luggage, 32–33
- code sharing, 16–17
- comfort, 91, 225–226
- complaints, 64–65
- differences among, 12–13
- discounts, 7–8
- flight cancellations, 57–59
- flight delays, 55–56
- food, 82–84, 206–208, 210
- in-flight systems, 85–86

Airlines (*Cont.*):
- information on, 5
- low-fare, 13
- nonstop/direct flights, 23
- on-time performance, 18, 57
- passenger courtesy, 66–68, 89–90
- rankings, 92–93
- safety concerns, 93–95
- seat assignments, 23
- seats, 79–82, 93–94
- telephones on, 145–146
- traveler's rights, 54–55
- upgrades, 66

Airport clubs, 68
Airport codes, 63–64
Airport Transit Guide, 43
Airporter, 41
Airports, 53–54
- alternate, 15–16, 162
- getting to/from, 37–51
- parking, 42–43, 69, 71, 113–115
- restaurants, 208–209
- security, 73–74

Alamo car rental, 102–103
Alaska Airlines, 145, 166
Alitalia, 81
America West Airlines, 145, 166
American Airlines, 82–83, 89, 145, 160, 166, 207
American Association of Retired Persons, 118
American Automobile Association, 110, 118, 188
American Express, 186–187
American Heart Association, 228

American Motorists Association, 112
Asia de Cuba restaurant, 50–51
AT&T, 141, 143–144, 148, 218
AT&T Wireless, 145
Atlanta, GA:
  airports, 75
  rail connections, 40
Atlanta Journal-Constitution, 5
AutoExec Pro, 109
Automated teller machines (ATMs), 184
Automobile maintenance, 110–112
Avis car rental, 101, 103, 170
Axtell, Roger, 191

Back-to-back airfares, 14
Backpacks, 20
Baggage claim tags, 29
Baltimore/Washington International Airport, 15
Batteries catalog, 69
Bay Area Rapid Transit, 137
Bel Air Hotel, 171
Best Fares, 5
Beverly Prescott Hotel, 171
Big Apple Car Service, 40
Boarding passes, 23
Booking, on-line, 7
Boston, Mass:
  airports, 44, 76
  rail connections, 40
Brakes, car, 111
Breakfast, 204
Briefcases, 28, 33
British Airports Authority, 179
British Airways, 81–83
Budapest, Hungary, airport in, 48
Budget car rental, 101, 170
Budget hotels, 127–128
Budgetel, 128, 131–132
Bumping, 54, 59–61
Burbank Airport, 15
Buses, 41
Business cards, 20–21
Business deductions, 109
Business Travel News, 5
Business travelers, other, 6
Business-class fares, 11
Business-class seats, 80–82
Butler, Deborah, 222

Calling cards, 73, 140, 142–144
Car jacking, 115–116
Car rental, 170
  at the counter, 104–106
  companies, 101–102
  driving tips, 108–110, 113–115
  insurance, 107–108
  international, 110, 188
  rates, 102–104
Car services, 39–40
Carey Airport Express, 41
Carey Limousine, 40
Carry-on luggage, 32–33, 35–36, 89–91
Cash advances, 185–186
Cathay Pacific Airlines, 96, 98
CB radios, 111
CD players, 86–87
Cell phones, 19–20, 87, 108, 111, 144–146
Centers for Disease Control, 180
Change fees, 12
Charles De Gaulle International Airport, 46
Check-in luggage, 28, 33
Checkups, 180
Chek Lap Kok Airport, 99
Chicago, Ill:
  airports, 15, 44–45, 75
  rail connections, 40
Cities, from airports to, 38–43
Cleveland, Ohio, 24–26
  rail connections, 40
Clothing, choice of, 29–30
CNN, 4, 183, 198
Code sharing, 16–17

Codes, airport, 63–64
Collision insurance, 107
Color schemes, clothing, 29
Colorado Springs Airport, 16
Colwell, Steve, 123
Comfort, in-flight, 91, 225–226
Comfort Inns, 128
Complaints:
  airlines, 64–65
  hotel telephone calls, 141
  hotels, 122–123, 125
Condé Nast Traveler, 5, 215
Confirmation numbers, 22
Consortium rates, hotels, 119
Consulate, U.S., 179
Consumer Reports Travel Letter, 5
Continental Airlines, 81, 145, 158, 160, 166, 207
Corporate rates, hotels, 118
Courtesy, passenger, 66–68, 89–90
Credit cards, 17–18, 107, 166, 185–187
CUC International, 207–208
Culturgrams, 190
CyberDocs, 227

Dallas/Fort Worth International Airport, 16, 209
Damaged luggage, 54, 62
Days Inn, 127–128, 132
Debit cards, 17–18
Deep venous thrombosis, 225
Dehydration, 225
Delta Airlines, 94, 138, 145, 158, 166, 208, 210
Denver, Col., airports in, 16, 77
Denver International Airport, 16
Departure fees, 17
Diarrhea, 181
Digital passports, 177–178
Diners Club, 186–187
Dining à la Card, 207
Dining programs, 207–208
Direct dialing, 140–141
Direct flights, 23
Discount airfares, 7–8, 11–12
Discounted coach fares, 10–11
Discounts, on-line, 7–8, 103
Doctors, 227
Documents, photocopies of, 178
Dollar car rental, 102
Dollars, U.S., 185
Door locks, hotels, 135
Do's and Taboos, 191
Driver licenses, 105–106, 110
Dulles International Airport, 15

Earplanes, 85
Ears, and air pressure, 84–85
Econo-Lodge, 128
Economy hotels, 127–128, 131–132
Edmonton International Airport, 75
"800" service, 140, 146–147
El Al, 94
Elite levels, 157–158
Embassy, U.S., 179
Ethnic restaurants, 210–211
Euros, 187
Exchange rates, 184–185
Exercise regimens, 227–229
Exit row seats, 80
Expiring miles, 166–167
Extended Stay America, 129
Extended-stay hotels, 128–129

Family, separation from, 218–222
Fear of Flying Clinic, 89
Federal Aviation Administration, 33, 80
Federal Communications Commission, 141, 144
Fees:
  calling cards, 142, 144

Fees (*Cont.*):
- car rental, 103
- departure, 17
- hotel, 123
- hotel room telephones, 140–142

Fire escapes, 133
First-class fares, 11
First-class seats, 80–82
Fitness, physical, 225–229
Fitness Guide, 228
Flight cancellations, 57–59
Flight delays, 55–56
Fodor's Travel Planner, 203
Follow-up notes, 20
Foreign money, 185, 187
Fort Lauderdale International Airport, 16
Frankfurt International Airport, 47
Frequent Flyer, 5, 165
Frequent Flyer Services, 156–157
Frequent traveler programs, 8, 23, 155–156, 169–172
- account status, 163
- affinity charge cards, 166
- concentrating on few programs, 157–158
- credit cards vs. debit cards, 18
- end-of-year activities, 159–160
- expiring miles, 166–167
- and high fares, 16
- information on, 5–6, 156–157
- partner programs, 164–165
- redeeming miles, 160–163
- taxes on, 167–168
- and upgrades, 163–164

Front-desk clerks, 121
Full-coach fares, 11
Full-grain leather luggage, 28

Gate agents, 66–67
Gate-checked luggage, 33
Gatwick International Airport, 45–46
Gray Line, 41
GTE Airfone, 145–146

Hampton Inns, 127, 131
Hartsfield International Airport, 75, 209
Health concerns:
- doctors, 227
- exercise regimens, 227–229
- fitness tips, 225–226
- international travel, 179–183
- jet lag, 229–231
- stress management, 223–225

Heathrow International Airport, 45, 76
Hepatitis A, 182
Hepatitis B, 183
Hertz car rental, 101, 103, 106, 170
Hidden-city airfares, 14
Hilton Hotels, 127, 130, 165
HIV infection, 181–183
Hobby Airport, 16
Holiday Inn, 127
Holiday Inn Express, 128, 132
Hong Kong, China, 96–99
Hopkins Airport, 24
Hotel consolidators, 118–119
Hotel Docs, 227
Hotel Reservations Network, 119
Hotel shuttles, 41–42
Hotels, 113, 117–118, 170–171
- alternate, 129
- complaints, 122–123, 125
- eating at, 211–212
- fees, 123
- frequent guest programs, 165
- front-desk clerks, 121–122
- inquiries about, 134–135
- international, 187–188

Hotels (*Cont.*):
minibars, 205–206
no rooms, 120
rates, 118–120
room telephones, 125, 139–142
safety, 133–134
special needs, 129–130
in suburbs, 130–133
types, 126–129
wrong, 120–121
Houston Intercontinental Airport, 16
Howard Johnson, 127
Hub cities, 14, 158–159
Hyatt Hotels, 127, 165, 217
Hyatt Travel Futures Project, 224

Immigration and Naturalization Service, 177–178
Immunizations, 180
Information, travel, 3–7, 38, 43
InsideFlyer, 5, 156
INSPASS, 177–178
Insurance:
car rental, 107–108
medical evacuation, 180
valuation, 31, 63
Inter-Continental, 127
International driving permits, 110, 188
International Foundation of Airline Passenger Associations, 94
International travel, 173–174
car rental, 110, 188
costs, 193–194
financial instruments, 183–187
health concerns, 179–183
hotels, 187–188
information on, 188–192
INSPASS, 177–178
interpreters, 189–190
laptop use, 192–193

International travel (*Cont.*):
passports, 174–176
planning for, 178–179
safety concerns, 195–196
telephone calls, 147–148
visas, 176–177
weather conditions, 183
by women, 194–195
Internet. (*see* World Wide Web)
Interpreters, 189–190
Involuntary bumping, 60–61

Jet lag, 229–231
Jones, Ron, 224

Kai Tak Airport, 99
Kennedy International Airport, 16
Kingsford-Smith International Airport, 48, 214
KLM, 81

La Guardia Airport, 16, 44
La Quinta, 128, 131
Laptop computers, 28, 33–35, 69–71, 86–87, 192–193
Late arrival guarantees, 123
Laundry services, 29
Leading Hotels of the World, 126
Leather luggage, 27–28
Left luggage, 34
Logan International Airport, 44, 76, 209
London, England, airports in, 45–46, 76
Long Beach Airport, 15
Long-distance calls, 140–141
Los Angeles, Calif., 169–172
airports, 15, 43–44
Los Angeles International Airport, 15, 43–44, 169–170, 209

Los Angeles Times, 4–5
Lost luggage, 54, 61–63
Love Field, 16
Low-fare airlines, 13
Lufthansa, 47, 81, 94, 210
Luggage, 20
  carry-on, 32–33, 35–36, 89–91
  check-in, 28, 33
  choice of, 27–29
  left, 34
  lost/damaged, 54, 61–63
Luggage tags, 29, 63–64, 72
Luxury hotels, 126

Magazines, travel, 5
Mandarin Oriental Hotel, 136–137
Maps, 114
Marriott, 127, 129–130, 155, 198
Marriott Courtyard, 127, 131
Marriott Fairfield Inns, 128, 132
MasterCard, 186
MCI, 141, 143–144, 148, 199, 218
Medical evacuation insurance, 180
Medical help, 227
Medication, 31, 180, 231
Merker, Kyle, 228
Metal detectors, 70
Mexico City, Mexico, 197–199
Mexico City International Airport, 47–50
Miami International Airport, 16, 75
Microtel, 128, 132
Midway Airport, 15
Midwest Express Airlines, 83, 166
Milwaukee International Airport, 15
Minibars, hotel, 205–206
Moderate hotels, 127, 131
Mondrian Hotel, 171
Moscow, Russia, airport in, 48
Motels, 134
Munich International Airport, 46

Name badges, 21
Narita Airport, 46
National car rental, 101, 106, 170
National Association of Professional Pet Sitters, 21–22
National Business Travel Association, 24
National Passport Information System, 175
National Safety Council, 88
New Tokyo International Airport, 46
New York City, 49–51
  airport buses, 41
  airports, 16, 44
  car services, 39–40
  hotels, 124–125
New York Convention and Visitors Bureau, 124
New York Times, The, 4
Newark International Airport, 16, 49–50, 209
Newsletters, travel, 5–6
Newspapers, travel information in, 4–5
Nikko, 127
Nonrefundable fares, 11–12
Nonstop flights, 23
Northwest Airlines, 81, 145, 166, 208, 210
Nutz and Boltz, 110–112
Nylon luggage, 27

Oakland, Calif., rail connections to, 40
Oakland International Airport, 15

Official Airline Guide, 5, 56–57, 60, 92
Official Frequent Flyer Guidebook, 157
O'Hare International Airport, 15, 44–45, 75, 209
Olympia Trails, 41
Omni, 127
On-time performance, 18, 57
Ontario Airport, 15
Orange County Airport, 15
Orlando International Airport, 75
Orly International Airport, 46–47
Overbooking, 54, 59–61

Packing, 27, 30–31, 33
Paris, France, airports in, 46–47
Parking, airport, 42–43, 69, 71, 113–115
Partner programs, 164–165
Passports, 174–176
Payless car rental, 102
Pegasus Fear of Flying Foundation, 89
Perrin, Wendy, 50
Petersen, Randy, 156–157
Pets, care of, 21–22
Philadelphia, Pa., rail connections to, 40
Philadelphia Inquirer, 5
Pickpockets, 195–196
Posture, 225–226
Prague, Czech Republic, airport in, 48
Preferred Hotels, 126
Preferred rates, hotels, 119
Premiere Worldlink, 148
Prepaid calling cards, 143
Preregistration, trade shows, 19
Prescription drugs, 31, 180, 231
Priority seating, 79–80
Public Internet access facilities, 70–71
Purses, 33

Qantas Airlines, 94, 215
Quality hotels, 126
Quikbook, 119

Radisson Hotels, 127
Rail connections, 40
Raincoats, 29–30
Ramada Inn, 127
Red Roof Inns, 128, 132
Refueling charges, 106
Regent Hotel, 215–216
Relais & Chateaux, 126
Renaissance, 127
Reservations:
- airlines, 10–11, 22–23
- car rental, 103–106
- hotels, 122–123

Residence Inns, 224, 228
Restaurants, 50–51, 171–172, 201–202, 214–216
- airline/airport food, 82–84, 206–210
- choice of, 104–207
- costs, 212–213
- eating alone, 211–212
- ethnic, 210–211
- information on, 202–204
- road food, 111

Road Warrior, 193
Ronald Reagan National Airport, 15, 76, 209
Rule 240, 56
Runzheimer International, 110

Sabena, 81
Sacramento Airport, 16
Safety concerns:
- airplanes, 93–95
- car rental, 113–116
- hotels, 133–134

Safety concerns (*Cont.*):
international travel, 195–196
St. Louis, Mo., rail connections to, 40
San Francisco, Calif.
airports, 15–16, 44
hotels, 136–138
rail connections, 137
San Francisco International Airport, 16, 44
San Jose Airport, 16
SAS, 81
Saturday night stayovers, 11
Scotch tape, 31
Seat assignments, 23
Seat belts, 94
Seats, airplane, 79–82, 93–94
Security, airports, 73–74
Sewing kits, 31
Sexually transmitted diseases, 181–183
Sheraton, 127
Shoes, 20, 31
Shulman, Ann, 123
Shutters on the Beach Hotel, 170–171
Singapore Airlines, 92
Sleep, 230–231
Sleep Inns, 133
Smoking ban, airlines, 54, 95, 229
Solomon, David, 110–112
Southwest Airlines, 35, 145
Special needs, 83–84, 129–130
Speeding tickets, how to avoid, 112
Sprint, 141, 143–144, 148
Stand-alone calling cards, 142–143
Stapleton Airport, 77
State Department, 175, 180
Stephens, Alice, 225
Stevenson, Robert Louis, 79
Stress, 222–225
Stuttgart International Airport, 47
Suburban Lodges, 129
Suburbs, hotels in, 130–133
Subways, 40
Super Shuttle, 41
Surrey Hotel, 50
Swissair, 94
Swissotel, 127, 210
Sydney, Australia, 214–216
airport in, 48, 214–216

Taxis, 39
Tel Aviv Car Service, 40
Telephones, 139, 149–152
calling cards, 73, 140, 142–143
cellular, 19–20, 87, 108, 111, 144–146
"800" service, 140, 146–147
in hotel rooms, 125, 139–142
international calling, 147–148
Terrorism, 196
Theft, 71–73, 195–196
Thrifty car rental, 102, 170
Ticket, The, 5
Ticketing, creative strategies, 13–14
Ticketless air travel, 8–9
Tickets:
airline, 8–9, 69
speeding, 112
Tires, 111–112
Toilet kits, 30–31
Tokyo, Japan, airport in, 46
Toll-free calls, 140, 146–147
TownePlace Suites, 129
Trade shows, 19–20
Trains, 40
Transmedia, 207
Travel agents, 9–10
Travel and Leisure, 5, 216
Travel Weekly, 5
Traveler's checks, 184–185
Traveler's rights, 54–55
TWA, 81, 145, 166, 207

United Airlines, 77–78, 83, 145, 166
Upgrades, 66, 104–105, 119, 121, 163–164
Upscale hotels, 126–127
USA Today, 4, 183
USAirways, 81, 145, 166

Vaccines, 180
Valuation insurance, 31, 63
Vancouver International Airport, 98
Vans, 41
Venice Beach Hotel, 171
Virgin Atlantic Airways, 81–82
Visa, 186
Visas, 176–177
VoiceNet, 148
Voluntary bumping, 60

Wall Street Journal, The, 4
Warsaw, Poland, airport in, 48
Washington, D. C.
  airports, 15, 76
  rail connections, 40
Weather conditions, international, 183
Weather problems, 58–59, 114
Westin, 127, 165, 210
Wheels, on luggage, 28
Wingate Inns, 131
Women, and international travel, 194–195
World Airline Entertainment Association, 86
World Wide Web:
  for international travel, 178–179
  on-line booking, 7
  on-line discounts, 7–8, 103
  public access facilities, 70–71
  travel information on, 6–7
Wrinkles, avoiding, 30

X-ray machines, 69

Zagat, Nina & Tom, 202
Zagat Airline Survey, 92
Zagat Surveys (restaurants), 202–203

About the Author

Christopher McGinnis is the director of Travel Skills Group, an Atlanta-based communications and consulting firm specializing in the business travel industry. It is his company's premise that *educated* travelers are happier, more productive, and efficient executives in the field.

In February 1997, Chris began working with CNN's Travel News Unit, and currently reports weekly on trends and issues affecting business travelers. Since 1988, Chris has penned popular columns for the *Atlanta Journal-Constitution,* and for *Fortune, Your Company, Condé Nast Traveler,* and *Entrepreneur* magazines. Before focusing on business travel, Chris was a management consultant and corporate trainer, logging over 100,000 miles per year.

McGinnis also creates and writes business travel newsletters for Fortune 500 corporations and for *The Ticket,* a monthly subscription-based newsletter for business travelers. His book, *202 Tips Even the Best Business Travelers May Not Know* (McGraw-Hill), released in June 1994, has sold over 35,000 copies.

Chris also speaks and leads seminars in the United States and abroad on business travel topics, and even offers training courses for novice business travelers who are about to embark on careers that require frequent travel.

He is a widely quoted expert in all major business publications (*USA Today, The Wall Street Journal, Business Week, Fortune, Crain's*) and is a regular guest on many business-related radio and television shows (CNN, CNN Airport

Network, CNBC, and Wall Street Journal Radio Network).

Contact McGinnis at TICKETATL@aol.com, or write him at: Travel Skills Group, P.O. Box 52927, Atlanta, GA. 30355.